WESLEYS AT OXFORD

WESLEYS AT OXFORD

The Religion of University Men

By PAUL F. DOUGLASS

1953

Bryn Mawr Press

PENNSYLVANIA

Manufactured in the United States of America by The Williams Printing Company, Richmond, Virginia, being set mostly in twelve point leaded Garamond type and printed on Warren's Olde Style White paper.

To my father

GEORGE C. DOUGLASS

who for forty-one years

served selflessly in the

Methodist ministry.

PREFACE

The portrait of John Wesley hangs near the entrance door of the great Elizabethan "Hall" of Christ Church in Oxford among those of the distinguished patrons and graduates of the royal college. From other walls of the refectory King Henry VIII, Queen Elizabeth, and Thomas Cardinal Wolsey look down upon the tables where the dons and students dine. The presence of this Christ Church man in such a celebrated company rests securely upon the historical importance of the awakening of a student's religious consciousness within the walls which enclose Tom Quadrangle.

Looking back at age sixty-nine upon his experiences as a student and fellow, John Wesley expressed the desire to be "again an Oxford Methodist. I did then walk closely with God and redeem the time." The emphasis on the Aldersgate experience in Methodism has long overshadowed a concern for the deep religious discipline which the Wesleys experienced in the academic environment and in the tradition of the Church of England.

This book seeks neither to be a complete biography nor a definitive history of the Oxford years of the Wesleys; it does propose to describe their religious methods. I have taken liberties with the materials to present, always with historical accuracy, techniques which may be relived by the sincere seeker. The book is therefore a manual of devotion developed from very human events in the lives of Christ Church men. Much of the material in this book has appeared in Zion's Herald and is reprinted by the courtesy of this oldest weekly journal of American Methodism.

PAUL F. DOUGLASS

Washington
District of Columbia

CONTENTS

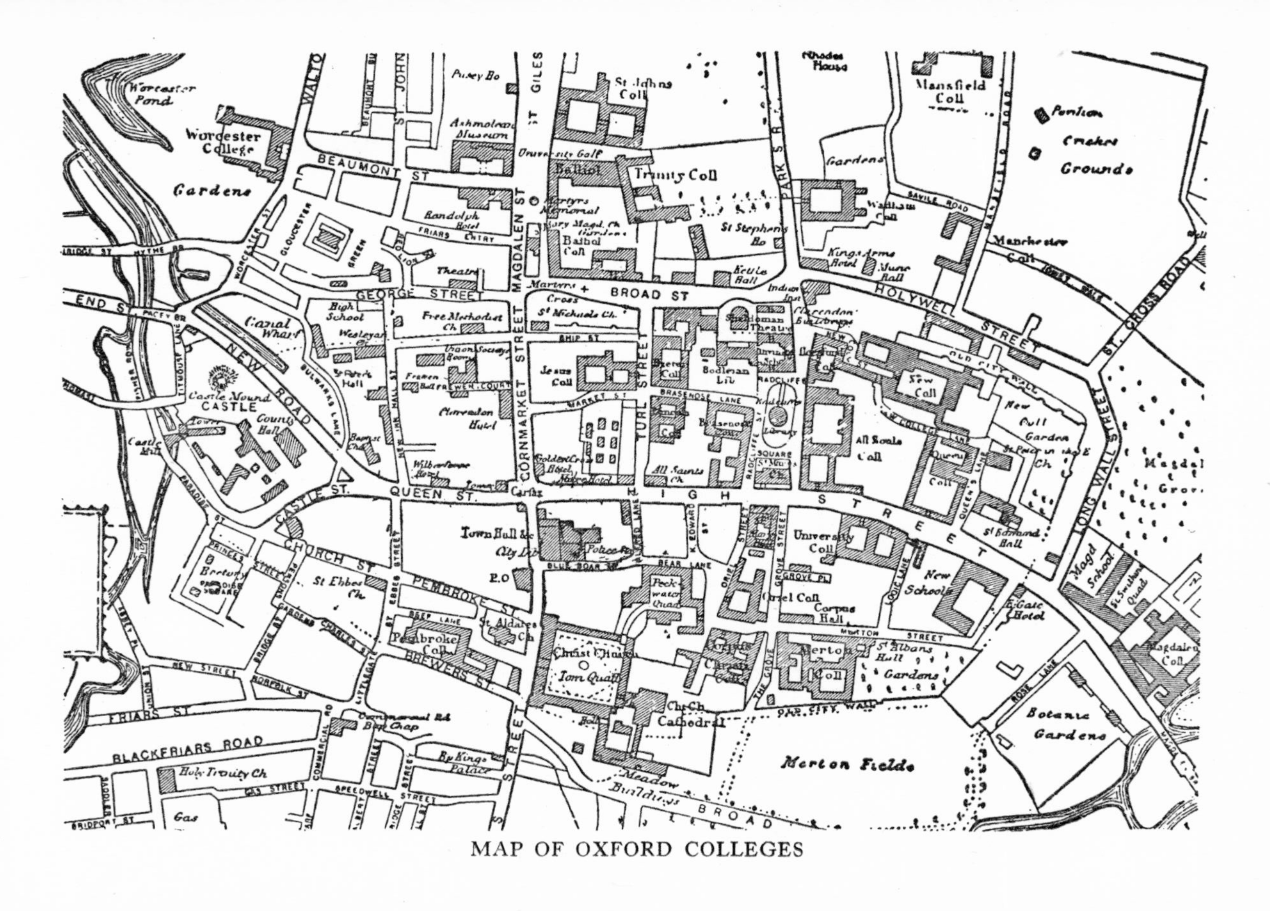

MAP OF OXFORD COLLEGES

WESLEYS AT OXFORD

GRANDFATHER

JOHN WESLEY

NEW INN HALL

1651

FATHER

SAMUEL WESLEY

Exeter

Master of Arts 1688

BROTHERS

SAMUEL WESLEY, JR.	JOHN WESLEY	CHARLES WESLEY
	Christ Church	
Master of Arts 1714	Master of Arts 1727	Master of Arts 1733

I

THE WESLEY FAMILY OXFORD TRADITION

John Wesley walked through the gatehouse into Tom Quadrangle to matriculate in Christ Church one week after his seventeenth birthday. To study at Oxford was a tradition among the men of his family. Grandfather John set the pattern seventy years before when he entered New Inn Hall. Father Samuel as a student in Exeter College took his master of arts degree twenty-three years before his first son, Samuel Junior, went up to Christ Church in the summer of 1711. When in June 1726 Charles Wesley at the age of nineteen marched over the Carfax and down St. Aldate's Street to enter Christ Church, he followed the example of his two older brothers. John had been elected a fellow in Lincoln College three months before.

Looking back across the thirty-eight years since he took his master of arts degree, the father advised his son, Charles, upon the threshold of his academic experience:

> "Never look back; for you know the prize and the crown are before you: Be not high-minded . . . Preserve an equal temper of mind under whatever treatment you meet with from not a very just or well-natured world. Bear no more sail than is necessary, but steer steady. The less you value yourself the more all good and wise men will value you, if they see your actions are of a price; or, which is infinitely more, He by whom actions and intentions are weighed will both accept, esteem, and reward you."

For most of the next nine years the brothers John and Charles lived within a five-minute walk of each other—up St. Aldate's Street, right over the Carfax at what is now the

Town Hall, down High Street past the Mitre to All Saints Church, and left on "The Turl" to Lincoln College. Companions in academic life, together they left the University to sail for Georgia on October 25, 1735, John, age thirty-two, to the Indians as a missionary for the Society for the Propogation of the Gospel, Charles age twenty-eight, as secretary to General James E. Oglethorpe.

During the near decade of their life at Oxford, John and Charles in company explored and practiced religion by method, seeking to possess and to exercise the mind that was in Christ. This book tells the story of the brothers as in these university years they explored ways to God.

APPENDIX TO CHAPTER I

CHRONOLOGY

JOHN WESLEY

1703 June 17	born	Epworth Rectory
1720 June 24	matriculated	Christ Church, Oxford
1725 September 19	ordained deacon	Church of England
1726 March 17	elected fellow	Lincoln College, Oxford
1727 February 14	master of arts	Oxford
1728 September 22	ordained priest	Church of England
1735 October 25	sailed for Georgia	missionary to the Indians

CHARLES WESLEY

1707 December 18	born	Epworth Rectory
1726 June 13	matriculated	Christ Church, Oxford
1733 March 12	master of arts	Oxford
1735 September 21	ordained deacon	Church of England
1735 September 29	ordained priest	Church of England
1735 October 25	sailed for Georgia	secretary to General Oglethorpe

II

CHRIST CHURCH

John Wesley took up residence in "The House," as Christ Church men call their college, when he was seventeen. His brother Samuel had taken his master of arts degree six years before; his brother Charles followed him six years later—all three brothers Christ Church men.

A college at Oxford consists of five functional centers of activity, (1) the residence dormitory, (2) the refectory known as "The Hall," (3) the library, (4) the chapel, and (5) the playing field. A student's closest relationships exist with his man-servant or "Scout" who attends him in his residence hall, awakens him in the morning, polishes his boots, and acts as father confessor, and his tutor who as his immediate academic companion stimulates and guides his intellectual interests. Men at Oxford live, eat, work, play, and grow together as a small group of active men. Intramural rivalry among the colleges of the University keeps spirits high. The college is the center of action; the University supervises the teaching not done by tutors, directs the research institutions, libraries, and museums, controls examinations, grants degrees, and regulates finances.

To fully understand Christ Church one must know its history. Christ Church is a triple foundation, (1) the only royal Oxford foundation whose highest officer is the reigning sovereign, (2) the seat of the bishopric of Oxford, and (3) a cathedral combining the endowments of the college and cathedral to create a single institution with the dean of the cathedral always serving as the head of the college.

John Wesley came to this historic institution as a student paying his own bills, that is, as a commoner with a stipend from his preparatory school, Charter House. Everywhere about him was evidence of the long continuity of Christianity from Roman Catholic beginnings to the priority of the established Church of England, from the simple piety of St. Frideswide to the secular vanity and rivalry of Cardinal Wolsey and King Henry VIII.

During the first third of the eighteenth century while the Wesleys were attending Oxford, Christ Church exceeded all other colleges of the University in its aristocratic prestige. Generously populated by lords, it had at the time an intellectual climate hardly equal to its social grandeur. A sporting young squire was advised to go to Christ Church if only for a term with the assurance that he would not have the least occasion to open any book there except such excellent volumes as the "stud book" and the "racing calendar."

When John followed his brother Samuel to Christ Church the college was still strongly under the influence of the cultured and genial climate created by Dean Henry Aldrich (1647-1710). Famous for gay life, splendid entertainment, and the love of tobacco and liquor, Dean Aldrich was the versatile and many-sided man. He could write with ease a textbook on logic or a treatise on heraldry, collect rare books and pictures, and compose with equal success sacred anthems and hilarious drinking songs. He could design a quadrangle, raise an endowment, or charm an audience inside or outside the Cathedral. He could write the chant *Jubilate Deo* based on the 100th Psalm "*O be joyful in the Lord all ye lands*," or as an architect draw the plans for All Saints Church.

When John Wesley arrived at "The House," Christ Church

was in the midst of an operation familiar to students of all generations; it was campaigning for money and constructing buildings. Ground had already been broken for the great library which Dean Aldrich had designed to replace old Peckwater Inn and to complete the fourth side of Peckwater Quadrangle. Huge in size and with gigantic columns, the new library, fifty-five years in process of construction, contrasted with the elegance of Peckwater but created the same effect of suddenness and contrast which Sir Christopher Wren's great tower produced in the severe Gothic Great Tower Quadrangle.

John Wesley saw the building blocked out; he also saw how institutions grow through the generosity of friends. Dean Aldrich had left his personal collection of books to the library, some thirteen thousand items. The dean's friends, following his example, in turn bequeathed their treasures to the library in their common desire to give Christ Church the "finest library" belonging to any society in Europe.

During the student days of the Wesley brothers, however, the working library collection of Christ Church was a congested affair located in the old Refectory of St. Frideswide's Priory. Brought up among books in the Epworth rectory, the Wesleys nevertheless used it regularly as they did also the Bodleian which was up "The High," over "The Turl" and down "The Broad," six minutes walk from Tom Quad.

In the easy-going worldly life of the "House" the seventeen year old rector's son found little that was congenial. He took long walks along the river and down the towpath along the Isis to the south. He strolled up to Port Meadow which had been common land since Domesday. In company with other students, because he preferred never to be alone, he breakfasted, drank his morning coffee and afternoon tea, and mixed much light chatter with his refreshment. At the coffee houses he read the news, listened to and joined in the gossip, read the *Spectator* and other periodicals of the day for a fee of three pennies a sitting or one guinea a year, wrote home, and read books on various subjects including astrology. In the junior commons room at Christ Church he argued the usual subjects which concern undergraduates and developed a reputation as a conversationalist and debater.

John soon discovered how hard it is for a young man to be diligent in a university environment. He read light literature, plays, and books, gamed indoors and out, drank tea with friends, hiked on foot and galloped on horse, and noted in his diary what students have always felt in need of—*sleep*. In his book he scribbled "intemperate sleep," "immoderate sleep." An entry for days in September when he was twenty-two will show how he reported his own activities.

Morning. Breakfast with tutor.
Afternoon. Read The Gentleman's Library. Sat at the Coffee House. Idle talk.
Afternoon. Walked in Trinity Gardens. Sat at Burman's; disputed warmly on a trifle.
Morning. Was treated by Dichter at the Coffee House and Tennis Court. Collected Bennet. Writ out the *Duke's Funeral* for Mr. Burcomb; talked of marriage with Griffiths; walked round the meadow.
Afternoon. Walked an hour: writ my father; walked from five to six; went to Tatham's: sat at the Coffee House.
Morning. Breakfast with Burman; collected Bennett: walked an hour.
Afternoon. Collected Bennet: played two hours at tennis.
Morning. Breakfast with Burman: read Jane Shore.
Afternoon. Writ to my Brother and to N.
Morning. Breakfast with Burman: writ to Varanese.
Afternoon. Writ to Varanese: sat at home with company.
Morning. Read Clark and Ward.

Afternoon. Collected Bennet: compared Clark and Ward: walked out: drank tea with Mr. Rigby: talk of predestination. Sat at King's Head.

His letters home show the life of a typical college man. He was often short of money. He worried about debts. He wanted to get letters from his sisters; he could, as he said, still afford a postage stamp to reply. He was homesick to see his mother and his old prep school. He bought fruit "very cheap" and apples "almost for the 'fetching'." He was grateful to his father who "very unexpectedly" sent him in a letter a bill for twelve pounds. In these days he developed a pragmatic philosophy. "I have been so very frequently disappointed when I had set my heart on any pleasure," he wrote, "that I will never again depend on any before it comes."

In his letters he gossiped. He told his mother about the small pox and fever in Oxford. He consoled his brother Samuel who had broken his leg. He wrote his mother about the rogues in town, one of whom snatched the cap and wig from one of his friends while he was standing in front of a coffee house door. He recorded the escape of a prisoner from Newgate. He visited a haunted house three miles from Oxford. He noted the warm weather in December with flowers "blown as if it were spring." He discussed international affairs and was pleased when the King of Poland promised satisfaction for the riot at Thorn between Jesuit students and Protestants who were accused of sacrilege. He was interested in Spaniards who daily plundered British merchantmen as fast as they could catch them in the West Indies. He wrote home about the steeple which fell from St. Peter's Church, about fire in the Mitre, and about the Oxford chandler who murdered two men and wounded a third. He had curiosity about events happening around him.

Increasingly, however, in his letters he discussed *ideas* much as any sophomore begins to look at them. He began to forge the furniture of his mind.

First, he questioned Jeremy Taylor's idea of humility as the virtue of thinking meanly of one's self. Frankly, John felt it was not a virtue to think one's self "the worst in every company." A man who endeavors to please God is better than one who defies Him, he agreed, but "if a true knowledge of God be necessary to absolute humility, a true knowledge of our neighbor should be necessary as a fair basis of comparison. To judge one's self the worst of all men implies a want to such knowledge."

Second, he defined faith as a "species of belief" giving an "assent to a proposition upon rational grounds." "I don't think it possible without perjury," he wrote home, "to swear I believe anything unless I have rational grounds for my persuasion."

Third, he doubted the existence of "an everlasting purpose of God to deliver some from damnation" (predestination) because the idea excluded all those from that deliverance who are not chosen. "If it was inevitably decreed from eternity that such a determinate part of mankind should be saved," he argued, "and none beside them, a vast majority of the world were only born to eternal death without so much as a possibility of avoiding it. How is this consistent with either Divine Justice or Mercy? Is it merciful to ordain a creature to everlasting misery? Is it just to punish man for crimes which he could not but commit? How is man, if necessarily determined to one way of acting, a free agent? To lie under either a physical or a moral necessity is entirely repugnant to human liberty. That God should be the author of sin and injustice (which must be the consequence of maintaining this opinion) is a contradiction to the clearest ideas we have of the divine nature and perfections." He felt that "faith must necessarily at length be resolved into reason. *God* is true: therefore what *He* says is true."

Wesley was getting down to fundamentals. He was especially concerned with skepticism which denied the existence of sensible things. His line of reasoning was this:

(1) If all sensible things are material,
(2) then if it may be proved that nothing material exists
(3) it follows that no sensible things exist
(4) and that nothing material can exist.
(5) If no sensible thing is exterior to the mind, then the supposition of a sensible substance independent of it is a plain inconsistency.
(6) Since no sensation can exist but in a mind
(7) *ergo*, no sensible thing can exist but in a mind, which was the proposition to be proved.

Or again:

(1) Everything conceived is a conception.
(2) Every conception is a thought.
(3) Every thought is in some mind.
(4) Hence to say one can conceive a thing which exists in no mind is to say that one conceives what is not conceived at all.

Wesley said ironically that Berkeley had "in plain English" said "everything immediately perceived is immediately perceived . . . a most admirable discovery the glory of which I dare say no one will envy him."[2] Or again:

(1) All sensible qualities are ideas.
(2) No ideas exist but in some mind.

(3) *Ergo,* all sensible qualities are objects of the mind in thinking, and no image of an external object painted on a mind exists otherwise than in some mind. And what then?

Fourth, in letters to his father John concerned himself with the question of the origin of evil. He examined as two possible solutions two governing principles—the one good, the other evil, the latter being independent on and of equal power with good and the author of all that was irregular or bad in the universe. This was the "monstrous scheme of the Manichees" confuted by St. Austin. The plain truth, said John, is that the hypothesis requires no more to the confutation of it than the bare proposing of it since two supreme independent principles are next door to a contradiction in terms, "two absolute infinities," and "he that says two had as good say ten or fifty, or any other number whatever. Nay, if there can be two essentially distinct, absolute infinities, there may be an infinity of such absolute infinities." Wesley held that one may fairly account for the origin of evil from the possibility of a various use of liberty — even as that capacity or possibility itself is ultimately founded on the defectibility and finiteness of a created nature.

John was thinking his way through; he was maturing. He found encouragement in the association with his brother Charles and continuing clarification in discussions with his father and mother.

As Charles Wesley felt the pressures of the campus bearing down upon him he too was encouraged by his father. Father Samuel suggested that he find time every day for a walk and then concluded with this advice:

"Hold up your head and swim like a man; when you cuff the

wave beneath you, say to it much as another here did, 'Thou carriest Charles, and Charles' fortune.' But always keep your eye fixed above the pole-star; and so God send you a good voyage through the troublesome sea of life, which is the hearty prayer of your loving father."

III

ROMANCE OF COLLEGE MEN

Among college men women command special attention. In the spring of 1725 John at the end of his twenty-first year opened his first university romance. The object of his affection was Betty Kirkham, the daughter of a rector stationed at Stanton and the sister of Robert Kirkham, a fellow Oxford student in Merton College.

Calling Betty "a gift of providence," he found her intellectually stimulating, spiritually sympathetic. It was Betty Kirkham who suggested to John that he read *Imitation of Christ* by Thomas à Kempis. It was Betty Kirkham who stimulated him to study Jeremy Taylor's *Holy Living and Dying*. It was Betty Kirkham who set him to reading William Law's *Christian Perfection.* And it was Betty Kirkham to whom he wrote letters in the coffee houses morning, afternoon, and evening.

The friendship with Betty Kirkham drew John and his brother Charles into a cozy circle of families all closely connected with the Church of England and with the political and aristocratic life of the times. These congenial friends lived in the villages of Broadway, Buckland, and Stanton, a day's ride from Oxford. The towns ranked among the most beautiful in the English countryside. Sometimes Wesley lodged at the Broadway vicarage, sometimes in Buckland, but it was at the open gate before the rectory in Stanton that he reigned his horse. It was on the hill above the highway looking down on the village with its stone cottages, ancient cross, and old church that he spent a memorable autumn afternoon seriously conversing with Betty. It was to Stanton that John went for the Christmas holidays in 1725 with his university friend, Robert Kirkham, and remained into the New Year of 1726. A wedding in the Kirkham family added to the gaiety of the old-fashioned "merry Christmas" and when John returned to Oxford he honestly asked himself the question:

"Have I loved women or company more than God?"

The lively young group at Stanton sat beside the fire, discussed books and events of the day, played parlor games to pass away the long winter evenings, and danced and danced. John believed in dancing as a wholesome recreation and form of exercise. When he was at Wroot and Epworth he danced with his sisters on every available occasion and over this Christmas holiday he found in the art a great delight.

The company in the Christmas houseparty included Betty Kirkham, her brother and her two sisters, and Mary and Ann Granville. John met the charming Granville women for the first time and became attached to them and to their vivacious mother. Betty confided to John that she loved him more than all mankind except her God and King, but it was Mary Granville, a charming widow of twenty-four with an income, who stole his heart. When the houseparty was over, the young men and women continued their friendship by forming a correspondence circle. According to the fashion of the day they gave themselves unusual names lightly to veil their identity and to add a halo of romantic color to their association. Betty Kirkham became *Varanese,* Mary Granville, *Aspasia,* Ann Granville, *Selima,* John Wesley, *Cyrus,* and Charles Wesley, *Araspes.*

The affair between John Wesley and Mary Granville, in

which all the members of the correspondence circle played a sympathetic part, developed rapidly. It brought together two persons of mutual attraction but two who were moving in opposite directions in life. John Wesley was entering the period of his richest religious experience as an Oxford student. Mary Granville was at her prime in the love of the world. If John found in Mary something of the world which was crowded from his own life by his religious discipline, Mary found in John's religious concern something of her conscience and something of the depth and stability for which she longed. Mary found John cute and intriguing; John found Mary glamorous and tantalizing.

When Mary heard John preach, even on a subject as remote from romance as *Primitive Christianity,* she asked him for his manuscript. John complied by laboriously transcribing the sermon longhand with his quill pen. When he transmitted the sermon, he told Mary about the "soft emotion" with which he glowed when he thought of himself as conversing with a kindred soul. When Mary thanked him for sending the sermon, she remembered the delightful conversation to which he referred and hoped it would "soon be renewed." John replied by recalling how beautiful Mary looked in the faint light of the "moon glimmering through the trees" in the garden where they were walking. John sent to Mary translations of hymns which he was making and Mary expressed the hope that the translation was "as near the office as the language" would bear. John wanted to get more letters and so did Mary but Mary was the more careless correspondent. "Take me into your protection," she wrote to John. "Look on me as one surrounded by infirmities and imperfections who flies to you for assistance against the assaults of vanity and passion. If you are desirous I should think of you as my friend, let this be the trial of it: not to leave any of my follies unreproved." John recommended a book, but Mary responded that she would "wait with impatience for the abstract you promised me which I am sure will deserve the time I may bestow in reading it." While John practiced the methods of religion, Mary was painting and drawing, going to operas and concerts, and enjoying the social life of London.

In the autumn Mary wrote to John that she with her mother and sister was leaving Gloucester on a Monday; she hoped to be in Oxford on Tuesday en route to London. John and Charles took the hint, met the coach at Burford, and rode with the Granville family to Oxford. Mary scribbled from New Bond Street in London that the conversation of John and Charles in the coach and the entertainment they had on the road to Oxford were so enjoyable that neither "the dirty way nor the rattling wheels" had any effect on the "pleasure of the trip."

Mary, however, was always in a hurry. She said that the life of noise and vanity in London could not possibly afford any entertainment to John Wesley, but that when she had the chance to converse with a "reasonable friend," she wished John and Charles were added to the company. Mary then confessed to John that she had been to two operas, had enjoyed them very much, and hoped that it was not a fault to be "transported by music." If it were, she said, she would try to correct her error. She apologized for sending a blotted piece of paper; she gave as her excuse "I am in haste." John moved forward. "Oh that our friendship might be built on so firm a foundation," he replied. "Were it possible for you to find me any way of repaying part of the good I experience from you, then I would not dare to doubt but I should experience it still but would still have some place in your thoughts."

Seven months passed; John received no letter from Mary. "I have a desire to recommend myself to your esteem," he wrote in expressing disappointment at her neglect of him. John wrote a second time; Mary now replied that she had been "in haste," that her eyes were weak, that she was afraid she would strain them if she wrote, that she had received all his letters, thank you. She added that when John came to London she hoped he would give her due warning because she and her sister might be "engaged with company that would not be agreeable to John."

John, however, looked upon the letter as an invitation and at once arranged to go to London for the Feast of Westminster. He told Mary to fix any day after the observance when he might call. She made an appointment for John and Charles to call on a Saturday afternoon between five and eight, but warned that she and her sister had to go out for supper. "We are," she said, "sorry to stint your time but we have been engaged sometime and can't very well break off. I am in great haste." When the time came, Mary cancelled the appointment on account of her sister Ann's health and moved the appointment up to Monday "for an hour or two."

Back at Oxford, John wrote Mary that London was the worst place on earth for preserving a Christian temper. He said how delighted he would be to talk to her for hours about the problem of trying to set her affections on things that "are above and not things that are in the earth." Mary, who was having a wonderful time in London, replied that the time with John and Charles when they called on her in London "was too valuable to forget."

When spring came Mary wrote John a letter from the heart. She considered how he employed every hour of his life either in his own improvement or in bestowing part of his knowledge on people placed in his care; she however was surrounded by vanity and impertinence and had fallen into the snare. She added that she didn't want him to think that she had neglected the book he sent her; she valued his recommendation "but the subject was too deep to be read in a hurry" and the next week she expected to have "time to read it and reflect." She said that every Sunday evening she was going out to a concert of music, as a matter of fact was going right out when she finished the letter. She wanted to know if John thought it an error to go.

This was the kind of leading question which opened up the field for John. He pointed out that to judge whether any action was lawful on Sunday the real test was this: does it advance the end to which the day was ordained? "Now the end to which the Sabbath is ordained," he argued, "is holiness. Whatever therefore tends to promote this act is lawful on this day. Whatever does not attend to advance it was not lawful on Sunday." He went on to say in his serious way that works of mercy are lawful on the Sabbath because they directly tend to advance the end to make us holy as God is holy. Works of necessity are lawful on Sunday, as also are works which "we ought to do but cannot on another day," and works "the neglect of which would obstruct the end of holiness." Unless concert going on the Sabbath promoted holiness, it was not allowable. John seemed to make it clear that gay Mary's pleasure in attending Sunday evening musicales was not conducive to holiness. Mary let the matter rest there because she enjoyed her concerts.

As summer came on Mary threw out another leading situation to John. She knew, she said, men of excellent understanding and learning and humanity and endowed with all agreeable qualities, yet to talk to them about religion and to listen to their opinions shocked her. These men of the world, she said, "allowed our Saviour to be a great prophet" but they divested Him of divinity. They admired the scriptures, but called "every part that mentions the Trinity fictitious." What did John think? Mary however was in a hurry, company was coming in, and she left the idea dangling before John.

John, back at Oxford from his delightful weekend spent at Stanton and Gloucester with Mrs. Granville, the mother, while Ann and Mary were in London—and sure that his visit would have been "added to" if the young sisters had been at home—now wrote to Mary in London that he wished he could "see her thoughts" once a month. Mary responded from New Bond Street, London, in mid-summer that she would tell him the real cause of her silence. Reason Number One was her brother; she was so happy in his company that her time was so consumed mornings that she found difficulty in getting time even to write home. Reason Number Two was that she was no housekeeper, seldom dined at home, often went with her uncles or with some particular friends who would not let her "spend a day home." Reason Number Three was that a gentleman and a lady for whom she had great affection took much of her time. They were in the process of going away from London, and she was helping them to buy clothes and furniture. She reported the bitter news that should John come to town she would not have the pleasure of seeing him because she was going out of town for some days. Yet she promised to answer his letters as soon as she received them although she "lived in a hurry."

John replied that in about eight days he was going to be in London. If he could not see her, he said he would the "more cheerfully bear my disappointment" since Mary had assured him that "now and then" she would think of him.

Mary at this point presented John with a case history for his advice. Because John liked to give advice, he went fully into the case. A young woman friend of Mary seemed to omit no duty either to God or man, yet she was discontented with herself and lived on the brink of despair. She felt she was in a state of ill health which perhaps contributed to her melancholy. Among her symptoms were coldness when she said her prayers twice a day and wandering thoughts. The week before she received the sacrament she suffered inexpressible agonies.

John responded. He regretted his inability to see Mary when he was in London, and proceeded to diagnose the case. The two symptoms of which the young woman complained, he said, were (1) inattention in prayer and (2) uneasiness before the sacrament. The remedy for inattention in prayer, he said, was to *pray oftener*. If she was praying twice a day, she should increase the number—pray three times a day. If she was taking Communion once a month, she should take it once a week. His theory was that God, seeing the earnestness of her heart, found the woman a "fit object for a large measure of His blessed spirit. As preparative he sends this pain (whether the immediate cause of it be in her body or mind) to cleanse her from all remaining sinful affections and to balance all those temptations that might prevent her from pressing forward to that degree of holiness which becomes them whom God thus delights to honour. If so, it will continue with her till it has had its perfect work."

In the meantime John had been again to the memory-rich Stanton-Gloucester-Broadway countryside. He had spent a pleasant summer day among beechwood trees on the crest of a hill on the south side of Stanton. From the rise he saw a beautiful view of the village nestling among the trees below and of the church with its graceful spire. In the distance hung the knolls between Stanton and Malvern Hills. More to the north and west were the fields and meadows extending through the valley of Evesham. Ann Granville had been home and she had asked John for guidance. He wrote her when he was back in Oxford that method related to her progress which would give the shortest way to knowledge was this:

(1) Consider what knowledge you desire to attain.
(2) Read no book which does not tend to the attainment of that knowledge, unless it be the best in its kind.
(3) Finish one book before you begin another.
(4) Read the books in such an orderly way that every subsequent book illustrates and confirms the preceding.

In concluding his letter to Ann he said:

> "I hope to retain some of the reflections of the smooth turf on which we sat, the trees overshadowing and surrounding us, the fields and meadows beneath, and the opposite hills with the setting sun just glimmering over their brows."

He hoped only that the next time Mary would be there.

Mary, however, was headed for Ireland. Before departure to Dublin she disagreed with John's diagnosis and prescription for the young lady's melancholy. She restated John's diagnosis that the young lady should add to the length or frequency of her prayers. Her friend, said Mary, had already tried that method and it almost killed her because of her intense application to her devotions. The real reason for her friend's condition, Mary thought, was "pride of heart." She pouted when she didn't get enough attention. Vain, she tried to rival her companions by dressing in clothes which she couldn't afford. With stern common sense devoid of any religious ideas, Mary concluded that if her friend could learn to be humble within the limits of her capabilities, she would be all right. In conclusion, Mary told John that she must for reasons of her own insist that he burn all her letters and that in addressing her in his letters he was not to use "any epithet before her name."

John nevertheless continued to discuss the young lady's case of melancholy. He summarized Mary's diagnosis of symptoms as (1) expecting great civilities from her acquaintances, with an aptness to think herself neglected by them, (2) a deep sadness upon the apprehension of their unkindness and the supposed loss of their affections which often carried her to such a length as to believe that God was forsaking her too, and (3) a desire to be equally well dressed as her companions, though she couldn't afford the clothes. What disorder is it, John asked, that causes these symptoms? The disease, he concluded, was *vanity*. The proper remedy was *humility*. So far now he was in full accord with Mary's line of diagnosis. The problem: *how to infuse humility*? Only God knows how, he added. With men it was impossible but Mary was probably an instrument of God's hand selected to perform this task. He concluded: "O Mary, how wonderful you are while you are employed in such offices as these."

"When I read your letters," Mary answered John, "I find myself carried above the world. I view the vanities I left behind with the disdain that is due them, and wish never to return to them; but it is my lot to dwell among them as yet. I will endeavor to defend myself from their assaults . . . With your assistance I hope to baffle and set aside their sting. But as from every evil we may extract good, so in this particular I have great consolation that, weak and insignificant as I am, I have sometimes found means of maintaining the honor of our great God when I have heard the blasphemer say 'Where is now their God?' At such an instant, how have I wished for a capacity equal to the mighty cause! for Cyrus' wisdom and words!"

John responded. "I would fain be nearer you; though I do what I can (alas! I fear not always) to overtake you." . . . "True," he said, "I have all the advantages given me that outward circumstances can afford. I spend day by day many hours in those employments that have a direct tendency to improve me. I have scarce any acquaintance in the world who is not either apt to teach or willing to learn; you are entangled among several who can plead for themselves little more than they do no hurt . . . Is it no hurt to rob you of that time for which there is no equivalent but eternity, on the use of every moment of which much more than a world depends?"

But Mary had gone to Ireland; she was in a hurry and had no time to write. John made the best of the situation by visiting her mother and sister Ann at Gloucester. Charles Wesley in the meantime had sent Ann a hymn which he had written at the age of twenty-four. Ann reported to John that her sister Mary had written from Ireland that probably by this time John had blotted her out of his memory.

Romances between young men and young women sometimes come abruptly to an end. The next summer Mary wrote John from Ireland. Her letter started like this:

> "I never began a letter with so much confusion to anybody as I do this to Cyrus. I can't recollect that I ever used anyone so ill and at the same time confess no one deserves it so little. I am so overcome with shame for what is past that I should not dare to put you in mind of my unworthiness. I give you now an opportunity of showing your forgiveness and generosity; not that you want extraordinary occasions to set those qualities in a proper light."

John replied:

> "I sincerely thank you for what is past—Adieu!"

The affair was over.

IV

FORMULA FOR HEALTH

Every young person faces squarely the problem of health. Physical stamina supports strenuous living. When he was twenty-one, John Wesley read what he described to his mother as "the famous Book of Health and Long Life—chiefly directed to studious and sedentary persons." The volume had been written by a physician at Bath named George Cheyne in response to a request from the master of the rolls for instructions to direct him "in the Conduct of his Health for the future and the Manner of Supporting his Spirits full and free." Dr. Cheyne's handbook was a systematic treatise dealing with air, meat and drink, sleeping and watching, exercising and quiet, evacuations and their obstructions, passions, and miscellaneous observations. As is generally the case in the publication of health information for the general reader, Dr. Cheyne incurred the displeasure of the medical profession, but as John Wesley observed to his mother in agreeing with the author, "doctors need not be afraid of their weak endeavors while the world, the flesh, and the devil are on the other side of the question."

The book began with the observation that "there is not anything that the generality of the better sort so lavishly and so unconcernedly throw away as Health, except eternal Felicity." Dr. Cheyne stated four basic principles for health which John Wesley adopted as a working code:

(1) *"'Tis easier to preserve Health than to recover it, and to prevent Diseases than to cure them."*

(2) *"You must eat less, or use more exercise, or take more Physick, or be sick."*
(3) *"The great Rule of Eating and Drinking for Health is to adjust the quality and quantity of our food to our digestive power."*
(4) *"Gentlemen of a sedentary life should use as much abstinence as they mildly can, consistent with the preservation of the strength and freedom of spirits."*

Adopt simple rules of abstinence, diet, and exercise, and forget about your health problem, advised Dr. Cheyne. Eat sparingly, drink lots of water—at least three pints a day—exercise and keep your circulation vigorous.

Speaking of people who keep worrying about their health, Dr. Cheyne said:

> "The reflection is not more common than just that he who lives physically must live miserably. The Truth is Nicety and Exactness about every minute circumstance that may impair our health is such a Yoke and Slavery as no man of generous free spirit would submit to it. 'Tis, as a Poet expresses it, to die for fear of dying."

The good doctor recommended riding as the most "manly form of exercise, the most healthy, the least laborious, and the most expressive of spirits." John agreed; he owned his own horse. The doctor further recommended tennis, dancing, and walking. John agreed. He was on the court almost every day, his dancing was in good form from constant practice, and he was fond of walking.

In emphasizing the importance of physical strength, Dr. Cheyne urged the proposition that

> "Without some degree of Health, we can neither be agreeable to ourselves, nor useful to our Friends, we can neither relish the Blessings of divine Providence to us in Life, nor acquit ourselves of our Duties to our Maker, or our Neighbor."

John Wesley agreed. Dr. Cheyne's health program for "full and free spirits" was effective, practical, and economical.

Equipped as a young undergraduate with these common sense rules of living which the Doctor said anyone could follow readily "without any trouble or constraint," John Wesley laid sound physical habits of living. His frail body became the instrument of a strenuous and useful life eighty-eight years long.

V

COMPOSITION OF POETRY

Young men often write poetry. Samuel, Jr., John, and Charles Wesley, indeed, came paternally by their urge to compose their thoughts in verse. Father Samuel in 1693 had written *A Heroic Poem on the Life of Our Blessed Lord and Saviour Jesus Christ* and dedicated it to Queen Mary. The performance led directly to his appointment to the living at Epworth. He followed this with a second work entitled *A History of the Old and New Testaments attempted in Verse and Adorned with 330 Sculptures.* If the father was not an inspired poet, he was at least an industrious one, and the boys followed his example. Charles, as he scribbled off more than six thousand devotional verses in his lifetime, produced some of the greatest hymns in the English language, and John in translating thirty-three hymns from the German channeled much of the richest hymnody of the continent into Anglo-Saxon worship.

The first record of John's poetry comes in a letter which he wrote on his birthday to his brother Samuel in the springtime of 1724. Samuel, recovering from a broken leg, found the verse enclosed in a letter written to cheer him in his confinement. John, translating from the Latin, said the poem took him an hour to compose and that it had one virtue: it was short. The poem read:

As o'er fair *Cloe's* rosy cheek,
  Careless, a little vagrant passed,
With artful hand around his neck
  A slender chain the virgin cast.

As *Juno* near her throne above
  Her spangled bird delights to see,
As *Venus* has her fav'rite dove,
  Cloe shall have her fav'rite flea.

Pleased at his chains, with nimble steps
  He o'er her snowy bosom strayed:
Now on her panting breast he leaps,
  Now hides between his little head.

Leaving at length his old abode,
  He found, by thirst or fortune led,
Her swelling lips, that brighter glowed
  Than roses in their native bed.

Cloe, your artful bands undo,
  Nor for your captive's safety fear;
No artful bands are needful now
  To keep the willing vagrant here.

Whilst on that heav'n 'tis given to stay,
  (Who would not wish to be so blest?)
No force can draw him once away,
  Till Death shall seize his destined breast.

John was no Robert Burns; but bad though his verse was, he enjoyed writing it.

As he studied Horace, John translated other passages into rhyme in the custom of language students of many generations. On the first day of spring 1726, he sent this verse from Book 1, Ode XIX, Horace, to Samuel:

The cruel Queen of fierce desires,
  While youth and wine assistants prove,
Renews my long-neglected fires
  And melts again my mind to love.

On blooming Glycera I gaze,
By too resistless force opprest;
With fond delight my eye surveys
The spotless marble of her breast.

In vain I strive to break my chain;
In vain I heave with anxious sighs:
Her pleasing coyness feeds my pain
And keeps the conquests of her eyes.

Impetuous tides of joy and pain
By turns my lab'ring bosom tear;
The Queen of Love, with all her train
Of hopes and fears, inhabits there.

No more the wand'ring Scythian's might
From softer themes my lyre shall move;
No more the Parthian's wily flight:
My lyre shall sing of naught but Love.

Haste, grassy altars let us rear;
Haste, wreaths of fragrant myrtle twine;
With Arab sweets perfume the air,
And crown the whole with gen'rous wine.

While we the sacred rites prepare,
The cruel Queen of fierce desires
Will pierce, propitious to my prayer,
The obdurate maid with equal fires.

Suffering with the spring fever of an undergraduate in correspondence with two beautiful young women, Betty Kirkham and Mary Granville, he made Horace's Ode XXII read like this:

Integrity needs no defence;
The man who trusts to Innocence,
Nor wants the darts Numidians throw,
Nor arrows of the Parthian bow.

Secure o'er Libya's sandy seas
  Or hoary Caucasus he strays;
O'er regions scarcely known to Fame,
  Washed by Hydaspes' fabled stream.

While void of cares, of naught afraid,
  Late in the Sabine woods I strayed;
On Sylvia's lips, while pleased I sung,
  How Love and soft Persuasion hung!

A ravenous wolf, intent on food,
  Rushed from the covert of the wood;
Yet dared not violate the grove
  Secured by Innocence and Love:

Nor Mauritania's sultry plain
  So large a savage does contain;
Nor e'er so huge a monster treads
  Warlike Apulia's beechen shades.

Place me where no revolving sun
  Does o'er his radiant circle run,
Where clouds and damps alone appear
  And poison the unwholesome year:

Place me in that effulgent day
  Beneath the Sun's directer ray;
No change from its fixed place shall move
  The basis of my lasting love.

The same spring John confided to his brother Samuel that he had at different times given five or six copies of his verse to an Oxford don and was going to receive from a friend more verse devoted chiefly to romantic notions of love and gallantry. To this point John's composition was an orthodox springtime undergraduate performance.

Again from Horace Book I, Ode XXIV, John sent the following poem to a friend whose father had died:

What shame shall stop our flowing tears?
  What end shall our just sorrows know?
Since Fate, relentless to our prayers,
  Has given the long destructive blow!

Ye Muses, strike the sounding string,
  In plaintive strains his loss deplore,
And teach an artless voice to sing
  The great, the bounteous, now no more!

For him the Wise and Good shall mourn,
  While late records his fame declare;
And, oft as rolling years return,
  Shall pay his tomb a grateful tear.

Ah! what avail their plaints to thee?
  Ah! what avails his fame declared?
Thou blam'st, alas! the just decree
  Whence Virtue meets its just reward.

Though sweeter sounds adorned thy tongue
  Than Thracian Orpheus wilom played,
When list'ning to the morning song
  Each tree bowed down its leafy head.

Never! ah, never from the gloom
  Of unrelenting Pluto's sway
Could the thin shade again resume
  Its ancient tenement of clay.

Indulgent Patience! heav'n-born guest!
  Thy healing wings around display:
Thou gently calm'st the stormy breast
  And driv'st the tyrant Grief away.

Corroding Care and eating Pain
  By just degrees thy influence own;
And lovely lasting Peace again
  Resume her long-deserted throne.

His pen shifted quickly to the object of young men's fancy.

By a cool fountain's flow'ry side
  The fair Celinda lay;
Her looks increased the summer's pride,
  Her eyes the blaze of day.

Quick through the air to this retreat
  A bee industrious flew,
Prepared to rifle every sweet
  Under the balmy dew.

Drawn by the fragrance of her breath,
  Her rosy lips he found;
There in full transport sucked in death,
  And dropt upon the ground.

Enjoy, blest bee, enjoy thy fate,
  Nor at thy Fall repine;
Each god would quit his blissful state,
  To share a death like thine.

With this kind of practice John advanced to tackle substantial tasks in translating into verse the second Georgic and paraphrasing in poetry the 65th Psalm. He was beginning to collect verses which expressed man's worship of God. The method of paraphrasing psalms and setting them to verse came to be for John a *method* of studying the scriptures for their deeper meaning and expressing that meaning in his own language. His manuscript transcribing the first eighteen verses of the 104th Psalm represents both his method and his result:

KING JAMES VERSION	Verse	JOHN WESLEY'S PARAPHRASE
Bless the Lord, O my soul. O Lord my God, thou art very great; thou art clothed with honour and majesty.	(1)	*Unborne aloft on vent'rous wing,* *While, spurning earthly themes, I soar,* *Through paths untrod before,* *What God, what seraph shall I sing?* *Whom but thee should I proclaim,* *Author of this wond'rous frame?* *Eternal uncreated Lord,* *Enshrin'd in glory's radiant blaze!* *At whose prolific voice, whose potent word,* *Commanded, nothing swift retir'd, and worlds began their race.*
Who coverest thyself with light as with a garment; who stretchest out the heavens like a curtain:	(2)	*Thou, brooding o'er the realms of night,* *Th' unbottom'd infinite abyss,* *Bad'st the deep her rage surcease,* *And said'st let there be light!* *Aethereal light thy call obey'd,* *Glad she left her native shade,* *Through the wide void her living waters past;* *Darkness turn'd his murmuring head,* *Resign'd the reins, and trembling fled;* *The crystal waves roll'd one, and filled the ambient waste.*
	(2)	*In light, effulgent robe, array'd,* *Thou left'st the beauteous realms of day!* *The golden towers inclin'd their head,* *As their Sov'reign took his way.*
Who layeth the beams of his chambers in the waters: who maketh the clouds his chariot: who walketh upon the wings of the wind:	(3) (4)	*The all-encircling bounds (a shining train,* *Minist'ring flames around him flew)* *Through the vast profound he drew,* *When lo! sequacious to his fruitful hand,* *Heaven o'er the uncolor'd void, her azure curtain threw.*
Who maketh his angels spirits; his ministers a flaming fire:		*Lo! marching o'er the empty space,* *The fluid stores in order rise* *With adamantine chains of liquid glass,* *To bind the new-born fabric of the skies.*

(3) *Downward the Almighty Builder rode,*
Old Chaos groan'd beneath the God,
Sable clouds his pompous car,
Harnest winds before him ran,
Proud to wear their Maker's chain,
And told, with hoarse-resounding voice, his coming from afar.

Who laid the foundations of the earth, that it should not be removed for ever.

(5) *Embryon earth the signal knew,*
And rear'd from night's dark womb her infant head,

Thou coveredst it with the deep as with a garment: the waters stood above the mountains.

(6) *Though yet prevailing waves her hills o'erspread*
And stain'd their sickly face with pallid hue.

At thy rebuke they fled; at the voice of thy thunder they hasted away.

(7) *But when loud thunders the pursuit began,*
Back the affrighted spoilers ran;
In vain aspiring hills opposed their race.

They go up by the mountains; they go down by the valleys unto the place which thou has founded for them.

(8) *O'er hills and vales with equal haste,*
The flying squadrons past,
Till safe within the walls of their appointed place;
There firmly fix'd, their sure enclosures stand,
Unconquerable bounds of ever-during sand!

Thou hast set a bound that they may not pass over; that they turn not again to cover the earth.

(9) *He spake! From the tall mountain's wounded side,*
Fresh springs roll'd down their silver tide;

He sendeth the springs into the valleys, which run among the hills.

(10) *O'er the glad vales the shining wanderers stray,*
Soft murmuring as they flow,
While in their cooling wave inclining low,
The untaught natives of the field their parching thirst allay.

They give drink to every beast of the field: the wild asses quench their thirst.

(11) *High seated on the dancing sprays,*
Chequering with varied light their parent streams,

By them shall the fowls of the heavens have their habitation, which sing among the branches.

(12) *The feather'd quires attune their artless lays*
Safe from the dreaded heat of solar beams.

<table>
<tr><td>He watereth the hills from his chambers; the earth is satisfied with the fruit of thy works.</td><td>(13) Genial show'rs at his command,
Pour plenty o'er the barren land:
Laboring with parent throes,</td></tr>
<tr><td>He causeth the grass to grow for the cattle, and herb for the service of man: that he may bring forth food out of the earth;</td><td>(14) See! the teaming hills disclose
A new birth: see cheerful green,
Transitory, pleasing scene,
O'er the smiling landskip glow,
And gladden all the vale below.</td></tr>
<tr><td>And wine that maketh glad the heart of man, and oil to make his face to shine, and bread which strengtheneth man's heart.</td><td>(15) Along the mountain's craggy brow,
Amiably dreadful now!
See the clasping vine dispread
Her gentle-rising verdant head:
See the purple grape appear,
Kind relief of human care!</td></tr>
<tr><td>The trees of the Lord are full of sap; the decars of Lebanon, which he hath planted;</td><td>(16) Instinct with circling life, thy skill
Uprear'd the olive's loaded bough;
What time on Lebanon's proud hill
Slow rose the stately cedar's brow.
Nor less rejoice the lowly plains,
Of useful corn the fertile bed,
Than when the lordly cedar reigns,
A beauteous, but a barren shade.</td></tr>
<tr><td>Where the birds make their nests; as for the stork, the fir trees are her house.</td><td>(17) While in his arms the painted train,
Warbling to the vocal grove,
Sweetly tell their pleasing pain,
Willing slaves to genial love.</td></tr>
<tr><td>The high hills are a refuge for the wild goats; and the rocks for the conies.</td><td>(18) While the wild-goats, an active throng
From rock to rock light-bounding fly,
Jehovah's praise in solemn song,
Shall echo through the vaulted sky.</td></tr>
</table>

Here is still one more example of his method in the paraphrase of the 46th Psalm:

<table>
<tr><th>KING JAMES VERSION</th><th>JOHN WESLEY'S PARAPHRASE</th></tr>
<tr><td>God is our refuge and strength, a very present help in trouble. Therefore will not we fear, though the earth be removed, and though the mountains be carried into the midst of the sea;</td><td>On God supreme our hope depends,
Whose omnipresent sight
Even to the pathless realms extends
Of uncreated night.</td></tr>
</table>

Though the waters therof roar and be troubled, though the mountains shake with the swelling thereof. Selah.	*Plunged in the abyss of deep distress,* *To Him we raise our cry;* *His mercy bids our sorrows cease,* *And fills our tongue with joy.*
There is a river, the streams whereof shall make glad the city of God, the holy place of the tabernacles of the most High.	*Though earth her ancient seat forsake,* *By pangs convulsive torn;* *Though her self-balanced fabric shake,* *And ruined nature mourn;*
God is in the midst of her; she shall not be moved: God shall help her, and that right early.	*Though hills be in the ocean lost,* *With all their shaggy load,—* *No fear shall e'er molest the just,* *Or shake his trust in God.*
The heathen raged, the kingdoms were moved; he uttered his voice, the earth melted.	*What though the ungoverned, wild abyss* *His firest tumultuous pours;* *What though the watery legions rise* *And last the affrighted shores;*
The Lord of hosts is with us; the God of Jacob is our refuge. Selah.	
Come, behold the works of the Lord, what desolations he hath made in the earth.	*What though the trembling mountains nod,* *Nor stand the rolling war,—* *Sion, secure, enjoys the flood,* *Loud echoing from afar.*
He maketh wars to cease unto the end of the earth; he breaketh the bow, and cutteth the spear in sunder; he burneth the chariot in the fire.	*The God Most High on Sion's hill* *Has fixed His sure abode;* *Nor dare the impetuous waves assail* *The city of our God.*
Be still, and know that I am God; I will be exalted among the heathen, I will be exalted in the earth.	*Nations remote and realms unknown* *In vain reject His sway;* *For, lo! Jehovah's voice is shown,* *And earth shall melt away.*
The Lord of hosts is with us; the God of Jacob is our refuge. Selah.	*Let war's devouring surges rise* *And rage on every side,* *The Lord of Hosts our refuge is* *And Jacob's God our guide.*

John's mother, Suzanna, was impressed by his compositions and wrote to him that she would not have him "leave off making verses; rather make poetry sometimes your diversion, though never your business." Charles in the meantime was also engaged in the undergraduate custom of writing poetry and sending his verse to charming young women in Evesham valley.

Samuel, Jr., in 1736 collected his verse into a 412 page quarto volume under the title *Poems on Several Occasions.* He dedicated the work to his kind friend and patron, Edward the second Earl of Oxford.

Out of the verse which the Wesleys wrote, translated, shared, and sang came in years which followed some of the noblest hymns in the whole literature of devotion.

APPENDIX TO CHAPTER V

FROM THE HYMNS OF THE WESLEYS

Samuel Wesley, *Father*

Behold the Saviour of mankind
  Nailed to the shameful tree!
How vast the love that Him inclined
  To bleed and die for thee!

Samuel Wesley, Jr., *Son*

Let yawning sluggards faint dislike display,
Who, while they trust tomorrow, lose today.

John Wesley, *Son*

Lord, I believe were sinners more
  Than sands upon the ocean shore,
Thou hast for all a ransom paid
  For all a full atonement made.

Translation from the German of
Nicolaus Zinzendorf

Charles Wesley, *Son*
THE COMING

Come, thou long-expected Jesus
  Born to set thy people free;
From our fears and sins release us,
  Let us find our rest in thee.
* * * * * * * *
Hark! the herald angels sing,
"Glory to the newborn King;
Peace on earth and mercy mild;
God and sinners reconciled."
Joyful, all ye nations, rise,

Join the triumph of the skies;
With angelic hosts proclaim,
"Christ is born in Bethlehem!"
Hark! the herald angels sing,
"Glory to the new-born King."

The Companion

Lamb of God, I look to thee;
  Thou shalt my example be;
Thou art gentle, meek, and mild;
  Thou wast once a little child.

Lord, I would be as thou art;
  Give me thine obedient heart;
Thou art pitiful and kind;
  Let me have thy loving mind.

Forth in thy Name, O Lord, I go
  My daily labor to pursue.
Thee, only thee, resolve to know,
  In all I think, or speak, or do.

The task thy wisdom hath assigned,
  O let me cheerfully fulfil;
In all my works thy presence find,
  And prove thy good and perfect will.

Jesus, my strength, my hope,
  On thee I cast my care;
With humble confidence look up,
  And know thou hear'st my prayer.

THE SUFFERING

Is crucified for me and you,
To bring us rebels back to God;
Believe, believe the record true,
Ye all are bought with Jesus' blood:
Pardon for all flows from His side:
My Lord, my Love, is crucified.

THE VICTORY

Christ the Lord is risen today,
  Alleluia!
Sons of men and angels say,
  Alleluia!
Raise your joys and triumphs high,
  Alleluia!
Sing, ye heavens, and earth reply,
  Alleluia!

Christ, whose glory fills the skies,
  Christ, the true, the only Light,
Sun of Righteousness, arise!
  Triumph o'er the shades of night;
Day-spring from on high, be near;
  Day-star in my heart appear.

THE MISSION

My gracious Master and my God,
  Assist me to proclaim
And spread through all the earth abroad
  The honor of thy Name.
  * * * * * * * *
A charge to keep I have,
  A God to glorify,
A never dying soul to save,
  And fit it for the sky.

To serve the present age,
  My calling to fulfil;
O may it all my powers engage
  To do my Master's will!

The Peace

Jesus, Lover of my soul,
  Let me to Thy bossom fly . . .

* * * * * * * *

Thou, O Christ, art all I want;
  More than all in Thee I find;
Raise the fallen, cheer the faint,
  Heal the sick, and lead the blind.

Thou of life the Fountain art,
  Freely let me take of Thee;
Spring Thou up within my heart,
  Rise to all eternity.

The Perfection

Love divine, all loves excelling,
  Joy of heaven, to earth come down;
Fix in us Thy humble dwelling,
  All thy faithful mercies crown!
Jesus, Thou art all compassion,
  Pure, unbounded love Thou art;
Visit us with Thy salvation,
  Enter every trembling heart.

VI

PRAYERS

Lift up our minds above all these little things below which are apt to distract our thoughts . . .

* * *

Compose our spirits to a quiet and steady dependence on Thy good providence.

* * *

Meet us with Thy heavenly grace . . . Stretch forth Thy hand and loose the chains wherewith our souls are entangled.

* * *

As we lay ourselves down to sleep, take us into Thy gracious protection.

From the spring night in 1725 when at the age of twenty-two he first read Jeremy Taylor on *Holy Living*, John Wesley composed prayers. He wrote them out with a quill pen—long prayers pieced together from models of classic speech to God which he found in the Psalms, in Jeremy Taylor, in the Book of Common Prayer, and in John Austin's volume on the *Ancient Way of Offices, Psalms, Hymns, and Prayers for Everyday in the Week and Every Holiday in the Year.* As editor and arranger, first as an undergraduate and then as a Lincoln College fellow, Wesley constructed and produced prayers as a *method of devotion.* After his return to Oxford from Wroot in the late fall of 1729, he compiled his prayers not only for his own improvement but for the use of the company of fellow students who were meeting regularly with his brother Charles.

In 1733 at age thirty he published a collection of these

prayers as his first book. He designed the volume for the use of his pupils and gave it the title of *A Collection of Forms of Prayer*. In the next twenty-two years the little manual went through nine editions. When John Wesley issued his collected prayers at age sixty-nine, he included these prayers of Oxford days! He never outgrew them.

A. John Wesley's System

When as an Oxford undergraduate John Wesley in his study above Tom Quad first read Jeremy Taylor, his style of meditation was fixed. It was formal, phrased in ritualistic words common to manuals of prayer. His language generally was smug in the pattern of Anglican liturgy, yet he sometimes fell into straight crisp Anglo-Saxon speech. At such times he used short native words and knit them together in a clear style represented by the sentences quoted at the beginning of this chapter. The important fact about his prayers, however, was that his practice of reading, copying, imitating, and adapting models of classic prayer was *a drill exercise,* a systematic method of devotional life which he developed as an Oxford student.

True to his own natural disposition for system, John assigned himself the task of writing a prayer for every day in the week and for the traditional festival offices of the Church around the Christian year. He tried to build into each prayer something of four ways of talking to God, namely something of (1) deprecation, (2) petition, (3) thanksgiving, and (4) intercession. With this basic formula he adjusted his emphasis to the calendar of the Christian year. He divided up the whole duty of Christians into five parts

(1) renouncing ourselves—*to show that we are not our "own proprietors"*
(2) devoting ourselves to God—*to recognize that "we are God's," that he is the proprietor of all that we are (a) because He created us, (b) because He purchased us by His Death*
(3) denying ourselves—*to refrain from some particular indulgence as a means of drawing nearer to God*
(4) mortifying ourselves—*to advance as a true follower of Christ by a constant exercise of self-denial*
(5) opening our hearts to the indwelling Christ—*to fulfill the law.*

B. Prayers for the Days of the Week

SUNDAY MORNING

Almighty God, Father of all mercies, I thy unworthy servant desire to present myself with all humility before Thee to offer my morning sacrifice of love and thanksgiving. Let the inspiration of the Holy Spirit assist me in all the duties of this sacred day. Take Thou the full possession of my heart. Raise there Thy throne, and command there as Thou dost in heaven. Being created by Thee, let me live to Thee. Being created for Thee, let me ever act for Thy glory. Being redeemed by Thee, let me render unto Thee what is Thine, and let my spirit ever cleave to Thee alone.

SUNDAY EVENING

Be gracious unto all of us whom Thou hast this day or at any time admitted to Thy holy table. Strengthen our hearts in Thy ways against all our temptations. Make us more than conquerors in Thy love. Send forth Thy blessed Spirit into the midst of these sinful nations and make us a holy people. Stir up the heart of our Sovereign and of all whom Thou hast set over us that they may be happy instruments in Thy hand of promoting this good work.

MONDAY MORNING

Make Thyself always present to my mind and let Thy love fill and rule my soul in all those places, companies, and employments to which Thou callest me this day. Let me treat all my neighbors with that tender care which is due to Thy servants and to Thy children. Preserve my parents, friends, and relations and all mankind in their souls and bodies. Forgive mine enemies and in Thy due time make them kindly affectioned toward me.

MONDAY EVENING

For Jesus Christ, His sake, graciously receive me. Accept my imperfect repentances and send Thy spirit of adoption into my heart, that I may again be owned by Thee, call Thee Father, and share in the blessings of Thy children. Refresh me with such comfortable rest that I may rise more fit for Thy service. Let me lie down with holy thoughts of Thee and when I wake let me be still present with Thee.

TUESDAY MORNING

May all my thoughts, words, and works tend to Thy glory. Heal, O Father of mercies, all my infirmities. Strengthen me against all my follies. Forgive me all my sins. Let me learn of Thee to be meek and lowly. Pour into me the whole spirit of humility. Fill, I beseech Thee, every part of my soul with it and make it the constant, ruling habit of my mind that all my other tempers may arise from it; that I may have no thoughts, desires, nor designs but such as are the true fruit of a lowly spirit.

TUESDAY EVENING

Thou hast preserved me from all the dangers of the day past. Under the shadow of Thy wings let me pass this night in comfort and peace.

WEDNESDAY MORNING

Set a watch, O Lord, over my senses and appetites, my passions and my understanding that I may resolutely deny them gratification which has no tendency to Thy glory. O train me up in this good way that when I am old I may not depart from it.

WEDNESDAY EVENING

Accept my poor services; pardon the sinfulness of this and all my holy duties; and bless me, my friends, and relations, my benefactors and enemies, this night and forever, with the blessings of Thy children.

THURSDAY MORNING

Help me with Thy grace that whatsoever I shall do or suffer this day may tend to Thy glory. Keep me in love to Thee and to all men. Do Thou direct my paths and teach me to set Thee always before me. Let not the things of this life or my manifold concerns therein alienate any part of my affections from Thee, nor let me ever pursue or regard them but for Thee and in obedience to Thy will.

THURSDAY EVENING

I give Thee my understanding. May it be my only care to know Thee, Thy perfections, Thy works, and Thy will. I give Thee my will. Whatsoever Thou willest may I will and that only. May I will Thy glory in all things. I give Thee my affections. Do Thou dispose of them all. Be Thou my love, my fear, my joy. And may nothing have any share in them but with respect to Thee and for Thy sake. What Thou lovest may I love; what Thou hatest may I hate; and that in such measures as Thou art pleased to prescribe me.

I give Thee my body. May I glorify Thee with it and preserve it holy, fit for Thee, O God, to dwell in. May I neither indulge it nor use too much rigor toward it, but keep it, as far as in me lies, healthy, vigorous, and active, and fit to do Thee all manner of service which Thou shalt call for.

I give Thee all my worldly goods. May I prize them and use them only for Thee. May I faithfully restore to Thee all Thou hast intrusted me with above the necessities of my life and be content to part with them too, whenever Thou shalt require them at my hands.

I give Thee my credit and reputation. May I never value them but only in respect of Thee; nor endeavor to maintain them but as they may do Thee service and advance Thy honor in the world.

I give Thee myself and my all. Let me look upon myself to be nothing and to have nothing out of Thee. Be Thou the sole disposer and governor of myself and all I have. Be Thou my portion and my all.

FRIDAY MORNING

Mercifully this day watch over me with the eyes of Thy mercy. Direct my soul and body according to the rule of Thy will and fill my heart with Thy Holy Spirit that I may pass this day and all the rest of my days to Thy glory.

O Jesus, poor and abject, known and despised, have mercy upon me and let me not be afraid to come after Thee.

O Jesus, blasphemed, accused, and wrongfully condemned, have mercy upon me and teach me to endure the contradictions of sinners.

O Jesus, clothed with a habit of reproach and shame, have mercy upon me and let me not seek my own glory.

O Jesus, insulted, mocked, and spit upon, have mercy upon me and let me not faint in the fiery trial.

O Jesus, crowned with thorns and hailed in derision

O Jesus, burdened with our sins and the curses of the people

O Jesus, affronted, outraged, buffeted, overwhelmed with injuries, griefs, and humiliations

O Jesus, hanging on the accursed tree, bowing the head, giving up the ghost,

Have mercy upon me.
Conform my whole soul
To Thy humble
Suffering Spirit.

O Thou who for the love of me hast undergone such an infinity of sufferings and humiliations, let me be wholly emptied of myself that I may rejoice to take up my cross daily and follow Thee.

FRIDAY EVENING

Father, accept my imperfect repentance, compassionate my infirmities, forgive my wickednesses, purify my uncleanliness, strengthen my weakness, fix my unstableness, and let Thy good Spirit watch over me for ever and Thy love ever rule in my heart.

SATURDAY MORNING

Thou art pleased, O Lord, by all Thy works and magnified by everything which Thou hast created. The sun rejoiceth to run his course that he may set forth Thy praise who madest him.

Nor do the moon and stars refrain to manifest Thy glory, even amidst the silent night. The earth breathes forth fragrance as incense to Thee, her sacred King. The deep uttereth her voice, the floods clasp their hands, and the hills are joyful together before Thee.

Thou madest light for our comfort, and broughtest forth darkness out of Thy treasures to overshadow the earth that the living creatures of it might take their rest. Fire, hail, snow, and vapor, wind and storm fulfil Thy word and manifest Thy glory. Suffer not the sons of men to be silent but let the noblest work of Thy creation pay the noblest sacrifice of praise.

Pour Thy grace into my heart that I may worthily magnify Thy great and glorious Name. Thou hast made me and sent me into the world to do Thy work. Assist me to fulfil the end of my creation and to show forth Thy praise with all diligence by giving myself up to Thy service. Prosper Thou whatever I shall undertake this day that it may tend to Thy glory, the good of my neighbors, and the salvation of my own soul.

SATURDAY EVENING

Though I am upon the earth, yet will I praise as I can the King of Heaven. Though a mortal creature, yet will I join my songs with immortal hosts of angels and archangels, thrones, dominions, and powers while they laud and magnify Thy glorious Name.

Holy, holy, holy, is the Lord of Hosts! Heaven and earth are full of His glory! Glory be to Thee, O Lord most high! Accept, O merciful Father, my most humble thanks for Thy preservation of me this day. Continue Thy loving-kindness toward me and take me into Thy protection this night. Let Thy holy angels watch over me and defend me from evil men and evil spirits. Let me rest in peace and not sleep in sin, and grant that I may rise more fit for Thy service.

PRAYERS FOR THE FAMILY

UPON ARISING

Come let us adore the Day-spring from on high. Let us live to praise and magnify Thy glorious Name. Give us that grace that we may duly examine the inmost of our hearts and our most secret thoughts. Now we stand before Thee: grant that we may this day begin to walk before Thee as those that are called to an inheritance of light in Christ.

UPON RETIRING

Day by day we will speak of the glory of Thy empire; and night after night will we utter the memory of Thy great goodness and of Thy tender mercies that are over all Thy works. Save us, good Lord, waking, and keep us sleeping that we may watch with Christ and rest in peace. Hear our humble supplication for the forgiveness of our sins. Hear us, O Lord, that we may live in peace and charity with all the world, especially among ourselves, united into one family, patiently forebearing, freely forgiving, and readily assisting one another. Keep us in safety under the shadow of Thy wings; for unto Thy Almighty protection we commit ourselves this night, humbly beseeching Thee that after due rest we may rise with thankful hearts and return with cheerful dispositions to the duties of our several vocations to glorify Thee by our good works through Jesus Christ our Lord.

VII

METHOD IN RELIGION

A. The Diary Record

Before John went up to Oxford as an undergraduate, his father placed in his hands a family heirloom. It was a small duodecimo book stoutly bound in half vellum. Its marble boards were time-worn, its pages yellowed with age. Three Wesley names appeared on it. The volume was transmitted from grandfather to grandson by the son and father. Now in the third Oxford generation John began to use it to keep a record of his doings and thinking and to plan and budget the use of his time. A student's diary serves as a useful and very personal document. It records the ideas he has bumped into and the little personal inventions which each young person develops for himself in taking hold on life. As his Oxford experience deepened, John's diary became an intimate record, a kind of mirror which reflected how he looked to himself.

As a general practice, John Wesley made his diary entries in code. The purpose of his cipher enabled him to economize in space and time and protected his record as a personal document for his own use. He used English, Greek, and Hebrew symbols with plenty of signs, numerals, points, and dashes. Letters were sometimes used in their natural and proper sense, sometimes one consonant in an ordinary word would be changed, and all vowels either omitted or replaced by full points. From time to time he introduced new ideas into his code writing.

B. Letters

The second "method" characteristic of John Wesley was his bent for personal communication by letter. The habit formed at Oxford was one of the effective instruments of his administrative genius. Often he noted dates on which he had written to particular persons in his diary; he also kept copies of letter, expressive of his own gregarious like for people. His letters during his Oxford days increasingly concerned themselves with ideas and personal definition of purposes. Commenting in later life on style in letters which he transcribed for the press, he said:

> "I think it my duty to see that every phrase be clear, pure, and proper. Conciseness (which is now natural to me) brings *quantum sufficit* of strength. If, after all, I observe any stiff expression, I throw it out, neck and shoulders."

C. Discussion of Ideas

If the diaries were personal documents, John completed the act of communication in association with others. Thought remains soliloquy until it is shared and milled over in face-to-face discussion and argument. In the junior commons in Christ Church, in the senior commons in Lincoln College, in the coffee houses, in walks with companions in Christ Church meadows, in the gardens of Oxford, along the tow path, in residence hall rooms, at holiday house parties, in conference with his tutors, as a tutor visiting with his own pupils—everywhere John "tried out" ideas, found which were soft and which solid. In the human interaction of companionship his gregarious nature found stimulation. It was the discussion of ideas that completed his circuit of communication. Entries in his diary show his habit:

"Walked in Trinity Gardens."
"Disputed warmly on a trifle."
"Walked around the meadow."
"Sat at the Coffee House."
"Sat at Lincoln."
"Sat at home with company."
"Drank tea with Mr. Rigby, talk of predestination."
"Sat at the King's Head."
"Talked of the nature of a Sacrament." . . .
(much harm is done by exaggerating the
venerableness of it . . . talked)

Sometimes he became quite formal in his presentation. To his brother, Samuel, he said:

"I had rather dispute, if I must dispute, with you than with any man living, because it may be done with so little expense of time and words. The question is now brought to one point, and the whole of the argument will be in a single syllogism: . . ."

The complete circuit of ideas which comes about by discussion exists as one of the most effective devices for making education "take." John Wesley used it to the full.

D. Wide General Reading

If the education of a student is aided by the diary, the letter, and the continuing discussion of ideas, wide general reading stretches the student's mind. A natural student has an "itchy" feeling for books and ideas. Often the ideas which most influence a student's life come from outside the student-teacher relationship. This was the case when Betty Kirkham suggested à Kempis, Taylor, and Law. Under his own momentum, moreover, John was not only reading the Spectator, current literature, and Latin and Greek classics, Hebrew documents, and French and English literature; *he was reading generally and widely "on his own."* In the fall of 1725 and the winter of 1726, when he was twenty-two, for example, he read a long list of volumes, threw in some plays and lighter reading, reread some, and "collected" those which had special meaning for him. Indeed during just one period of six months he read more than a book a week in addition to translating the fifteenth chapter of Proverbs into Latin verse and studying thoroughly the books of Ezra, Proverbs, and Ecclesiastes in the Old Testament and the gospels of Matthew, Mark, and Luke, and the epistles to the Colossians and Thessalonians in the New Testament.

E. Abstracting

Oxford has long required its men on examination to take passages of language and reduce the thought to brief statement. One of the most valuable skills which the Oxford man develops in this habit of analysis and restatement in the "collection." The verb "collected" appears over and over again in John Wesley's diary.

To "collect a book" meant to make a synopsis of it with notes and abstracts. The original purpose of "collecting" was to prepare for examination. "Collected" documents proved to be an effective technique for mastering the content of a volume. John acquired the habit early in his Oxford career. It appealed to his natural bent for method and system; the summaries turned out to be a convenient device for the circulation of ideas among his acquaintances. Mary Granville, indeed, proposed "to save time" by reading the summary which John "collected" in preference to the original.

John Wesley became one of the "best gatherers and scatterers of useful knowledge for adults that England knew." The beginning of this performance can be seen in these Oxford days when he "collected books." The *method* of systematic book review and analysis equipped him effectively to gather, digest, and put other people's ideas to work.

F. Organization of Time

At Oxford John learned the importance of planning the use of time. Toward the end of 1721 in his eighteenth year, he drew a time plan on the inner cover of his grandfather's notebook. In this proposed time budget he laid out his schedule of studies for 1722 with a plan for each day of the week. He listed the subjects which he proposed to take and outlined the order in which he would write to his father, mother, sisters, and brothers.

After he studied Jeremy Taylor, thanks to the influence of Betty Kirkham, he began to keep a more elaborate journal. "I began," he said, "to take *a more exact account* than I had done before of the manner wherein I spent my time, writing down how I had employed every hour." The strong influence of Taylor appears in the statements on rules for the use of time which John now wrote in his diary in such a way as to dominate the whole record. The rules for the most part represented a "collection" of Taylor's sentences which impressed John as he read them. These restatements exercised a continuing influence throughout John's whole life and work. The compact organization of the material is witness of John's capacity to "systematize" his reading.

His diary entries show that he not only stated the rules but that he also applied them to himself. Two examples will suffice to show his procedure in self-analysis. His journal for Friday, March 26, 1722, for example, shows this self-judgment:

"I found a great many unclean thoughts arise in prayer (or devotion) and discovered these temptations to it:

"a. Too much addicting myself to a light behavior at all times.

"b. Listening too much to idle talk, or reading vain plays or books.

"c. Idleness, and lastly—want of devotion—consideration in whose presence I am.

"From which I perceive it is necessary

"a. To labour for a grace and modest carriage

"b. To avoid vain and light company

"c. To entertain awful apprehensions of the presence of God

"d. To avoid idleness, freedom with women, and high-seasoned meats

"e. To resist the very beginnings of lust, not by arguing with, but by thinking no more of it or by immediately going into company

"f. To use frequent and fervent prayer."

While these thoughts show the strong influence of Jeremy Taylor, they represent very much the same observations which self-critical young men from Benjamin Franklin to a current sophomore have made. Perhaps more significant than the rules themselves is the style of English composition which John used. There are general headings, numbered statements, and alphabetical sub-headings. The *literary method* thus *shows an orderly mind* which could digest material and present it in organized form for personal study and use.

On December 1, 1725, he noted in his journal:

"Breach of vows: hence carelessness of fixing days of mortification, &c.

"Pride of my parts or holiness: greedy of praise: peevishness: idleness.

"Intemperance in sleep: sins of thought: hence useless or sinful anger.

"Breach of promise: dissimulation: lying: rash censures: condemning others: disrespect of governors: desire to seem better than I am."

G. Self-Inspection

From the days when he first read Thomas à Kempis and Jeremy Taylor, John Wesley knew that spiritual improvement does not come without systematic effort; *a person has to provide the time for self-inspection.* Following his ordination as a deacon in September 1725, John set aside Saturday night to hold an inquisition about his own religious experience and personal performance. The session was private, only John Wesley's soul and his Lord being present at the end-of-the-week critique. In his diary he recorded week by week his confessions and his resolutions—the results of his self-inspection.

Between October 1, 1733, and April 22, 1734, he pursued the self-examination to its superlative point. With the beginning of 1734 he adapted a new scheme to the already effective method for the nurture of a good conscience and the application of such an inner light in everyday life. His diary shows fine pencil rulings corresponding to the departments of his living such as secular, religious, intellectual, and physical. Down the left-hand margin of the page he entered numbers to represent the hours of the day from 4:00 A.M. to 9:00 P.M. A second column which he introduced with the letter "E" provided for notations about ejaculatory prayer, while a third column with figures down the middle of the page gave the entry for minutes spent at the close of each hour of devotion.

H. Exercise

As an Oxford undergraduate, John Wesley methodically developed habits of taking simple exercises. His entries in his diary show the informal way in which he took his relaxation from his studies:

"Was treated by Ditcher at the Coffee House and Tennis Court."
"Walked round the meadow."
"Walked an hour."
"Walked from five to six."
"Walked an hour."
"Played two hours at tennis."
"Walked in Trinity Gardens."

By diet, coupled with daily exercise in (1) walking, (2) dancing, (3) riding his horse, (4) rowing, and (5) playing tennis, he kept himself in shape.

I. Interrogations

John and Charles Wesley developed the "interrogative" as a means of questioning their critics. These interrogatives were an orderly series of questions submitted to friend and opponent alike to offer them opportunity to make specific answers to specific questions. This method of facing critics with the need for being specific is both a procedure in pleading at English law and a very potent device for getting discussion down to the facts of the case.

Here is an example of an interrogative submitted by the Wesleys to Oxford men who concerned themselves with the "follies" of "that ridiculous society" of which John and Charles were central figures:

INTERROGATORY

I Principles	*Answer*	
	Yes *or*	*No*
A. Does it concern all men of all conditions to imitate Christ, as much as they can, "Who went about doing good"?	☐	☐

B. Should a Christian act seriously on the command that "while we have time, let us do good to all men"? ☐ ☐

C. Will a man be happier hereafter if he does more good now? ☐ ☐

D. Will a man hereafter be happy unless he has according to his power "fed the hungry, clothed the naked, visited those that are sick, and in prison;" and made all these actions subservient to an higher purpose, even the saving of the soul? ☐ ☐

E. Is it our bounded duty always to remember that He did more for us than we can do for Him, who assures us "Inasmuch as ye have done it unto one of the least of these, My brethren, ye have done it unto Me"? ☐ ☐

II GENERAL APPLICATIONS

A. Should a man on the basis of these considerations, try to do good to his acquaintances? ☐ ☐

B. Should a man try to convince such acquaintances of the necessity of being Christians? ☐ ☐

C. Should a man so engaged improve his mind and concern himself with scholarship? ☐ ☐

D. Should a man to achieve either learning or virtue employ method with industry? ☐ ☐

E. Will frequent taking of communion persuade men to confirm and increase their industry? ☐ ☐

F. Should one person recommend to his acquaintances authors whom he feels have written best on various subjects? ☐ ☐

G. Should one person help other persons, as able, to form resolutions upon what they have read in those authors, and to execute them with steadiness and perseverance? ☐ ☐

III Specific Applications

A.	Should a man upon the basis of these considerations, try to do good to those that are hungry, naked, or sick?	☐	☐
B.	Should a man who knows a necessitous family give them a little food, clothes, or physic as they want?	☐	☐
C.	May a man give a family, if they can read, a Bible, Common Prayer Book, or *Whole Duty of Man?*	☐	☐
D.	May a man now and then inquire how the family has used the books; explain what they don't understand, and enforce what they do?	☐	☐
E.	May a man enforce upon them more especially the necessity of private prayer and of frequenting the Church and Sacrament?	☐	☐
F.	May a man contribute what little he is able toward having the family's children clothed and taught to read?	☐	☐
G.	May a man take care that such children be taught their catechism and short prayers for morning and evening?	☐	☐
H.	May a man try to do good to those in prison?	☐	☐
I.	May a man help with small sums to release well-disposed persons from prison?	☐	☐
J.	May a person lend another of any trade small sums to help such person procure tools and materials to work with?	☐	☐
K.	May one person give to those who appear to want it most a little money or clothes or physic?	☐	☐

J. Enthusiasm in Group Work

Within the busy life of Oxford the Wesleys became a part of a small "company" bound by an agreement to spend three or four evenings a week together. The little group began to crystallize in November 1729 when John returned from his year of assisting his father in the section of his parish which lay in the bog-surrounded village of Wroot. At the time Charles Wesley, John Wesley, and William Morgan, a fellow student from Dublin, Ireland, comprised the group. Their purpose was as congenial persons in a small group to pursue common objectives, to read the classics over together, which they had already read in private as preparation, and on Sundays to read some book in divinity.

The students met in one another's rooms during the winter of 1729-1730. The next summer, 1730, Morgan reported to the group that he had called at the jail to see a man condemned for killing his wife and that at the same time he had talked with one of the debtors. He said that he felt it would do the debtors a lot of good if the University students would take pains now and then to speak with them. Morgan kept repeating the idea until one August day John and Charles walked with Morgan down to the Castle where the prisoners were kept. So impressed were the brothers with the good of their visit that they agreed to go regularly once or twice a week.

It was therefore through the concern of Morgan that the Wesleys added social service projects to the "method" of their little company of university students.

John wrote his father about their visits. Samuel replied:

> "I have the highest reason to bless God that He has given me two sons together in Oxford to whom He has given grace and courage to turn the war against the world and the devil which is the best way to conquer them . . . I think I must adopt Mr. Morgan to be my son together with you and your brother Charles. Go on, then, in God's name in the path to which your Saviour has directed

you, and that track wherein your father has gone before you! For when I was an undergraduate at Oxford, I visited those in the Castle there, and reflect on it with great satisfaction to this day. Walk as prudently as you can, though not fearfully, and my heart and prayers are with you."

The father had only one recommendation—that his boys combat "the flesh" by "fasting and prayer." On December 1 Samuel wrote his sons again:

> "I question whether a mortal can arrive to a greater degree of perfection than steadily to do good, and for that very reason patiently and meekly to suffer evil. For my part on the present view of your actions and designs, my daily prayers are that God would keep you humble."

By this time the "little company" had grown to five persons. Its members were referred to in the Oxford colleges as "The Godly Club" and sometimes with more dignity as "The Enthusiasts" or "The Reforming Club." The fact was that a small group of students were methodically expressing *spiritual enthusiasm*. This expression of enthusiasm was more important than the methods by which it was expressed.

The pattern of the group was summed up by John Wesley in a letter to William Morgan's father, under three headings:

(1) Doing what good we can.
(2) Communicating as oft as we have an opportunity.
(3) Observing the fasts of the Church.

Taking the activities of the "little company" as a whole, one finds their principles to be these:

(1) A small face-to-face group of men with a common purpose becomes a sustaining fellowship.
(2) This group meets regularly on schedule.
(3) The group enriches its experiences by planned reading and digests ideas by group discussion and personal application.

(4) The members reinvigorate their purposes by taking Communion regularly and frequently.

(5) The members express their devotion through practical projects of service to others for whom they have an economic, political, intellectual, and spiritual concern.

As the "company" was developing its highest influence at Oxford, William Morgan was taken ill. In June 1732 he went home to Dublin and died on August 26. The intrusion of death into a circle of University men shocked the brothers and their circle of friends. Brother Samuel, deeply moved by the report, came to the immediate support of John and Charles. Taking his pen, he wrote a verse which expressed his feelings at the moment.

ON THE DEATH OF MR. WILLIAM MORGAN

OF CHRIST CHURCH

Who died August 26, 1732

BY THE REV. SAMUEL WESLEY, A.M.

We fools counted his life madness.

If aught beneath them happy could attend,
Let Morgan hear the triumph of a friend,
And hear well-pleased. Let libertines so gay
With careless indolence despise the lay;
Let critic wits, and fools for laughter born,
Their verdict pass with supercilious scorn;
Let jovial crowds, by wine their senses drowned,
Stammer out censure in their frantic round;
Let yawning sluggards faint dislike display,
Who, while they trust tomorrow, lose today,—
Let such as these the sacred strains condemn,
For 'tis true glory to be hissed by them.

Wise in his prime, he waited not for noon;
Convinced that mortal never lived too soon.
As if foreboding then his little stay,
He made his morning bear the heat of day.
Fixed, while unfading glory he pursues,
No ill to hazard, and no good to lose;
No fair occasion glides unheeded by;
Snatching the golden moments as they fly,
He by few fleeting hours ensures eternity.

Friendship's warm beams his artless breast inspire,
And tend'rest rev'rence for a much-loved sire.
He dared for heaven this flattering world forgo,
Ardent to teach, as diligent to know;
Unwarped by sensual views or vulgar aims,
By idle riches, or by idler names;
Fearful of sin in every close disguise;
Unmoved by threat'ning, or by glozing lies.
Seldom indeed the wicked came so far,
Forced by his piety to defensive war;
Whose zeal for other men's salvation shown,
Beyond the reach of hell secured his own.
Gladd'ning the poor, where'er his steps he turned;
Where pined the orphan, or the widow mourned;
Where prisoners sighed beneath guilt's horrid stain,
The worst confinement and the heaviest chain;
Where Death's sad shade the uninstructed sight
Veiled with thick darkness in the land of light.
Our Saviour thus fulfilled His great design
(If human we may liken to divine),
Healed each disease that bodies frail endure,
And preached th' unhoped-for gospel to the poor.

To means of grace the last respect he showed,
Nor sought new paths, as wiser than his God;
Their sacred strength preserved him from extremes
Of empty outside or enthusiast dreams;
Whims of Molinos, lost in repture's mist,
Or Quaker, late-reforming quietist.

He knew that works our faith must here employ,
And that 'tis heaven's great business to enjoy.
Fixed on that heaven he Death's approaches saw,
Nor vainly murmured at our nature's law;
Repined not that his youth so soon should go,
Nor grieved for fleeting pleasures here below.
Of sharpest anguish scorning to complain,
He fills with mirth the intervals of pain.
Not only unappalled, but joyful, sees
The dark, cold passage that must lead to peace;
Strong with immortal bloom, secure to rise,
The tears for ever banished from his eyes.

Who now regrets his early youth would spend
The life so nobly that so soon should end?
Who blames the stripling for performing more
Than Doctors grave, and Prelates of three score?
Who now esteems his fervour indiscreet,
His prayers too frequent, or his alms too great?
Who thinks, where blest he reigns beyond the sky,
His crown too radiant, or his throne too high?
Who but the Fiend, who once his course withstood,
And whispered,—'Stay till fifty to be good'?
Sure, if believed, t' obtain his hellish aim,
Adjourning to the time that never came.

VIII

THE INFLUENCE OF BOOKS

A very few books coming into the possession of a young person at the threshold of maturity have often impressed his life and shaped the course of subsequent thinking and doing. John Wesley came upon three such volumes in the spring, summer, and fall of 1725 when he was twenty-two years of age. Upon the recommendation of Betty Kirkham he began seriously to read *The Imitation of Christ,* a book written in vigorous Latin by a German monk named Thomas à Kempis. Although he had often seen the volume, a popular devotional manual, he had not studied it until the inspiration came from Betty.

John applied to the analysis of the book his own methodical procedures, "collected" and made detailed abstracts of its content, and took issue with some of the positions held by the monk.

A. Thomas à Kempis

In the characteristic way in which young men appropriate the wisdom of the ages to strengthen and improve their own habits of life, John extracted the substance from one section of the Thomas à Kempis volume like this:

FIRST BOOK

Admonitions Profitable for the Spiritual Life

(1) IMITATE CHRIST

"He that followeth me shall not walk in darkness." To seek true illumination and deliverance from all

blindness of heart, imitate the life and character of Christ. Dwell upon it. Strive to conform your whole life to that mind of Christ. All is vanity save to love God, and Him only to serve.

(2) BE HUMBLE

The highest and most profitable lesson has been learned when a man truly knows and judges lowly of himself. This is the great and perfect wisdom; to account nothing of one's self, and to think always kindly and highly of others. All of us are weak and frail but hold no man more frail than yourself.

(3) DO GOD'S WILL

The truly learned man is the one who, forsaking his own will, does the will of God.

(4) SEEK AND TAKE GOOD ADVICE

Take counsel with a man who is wise and of a good conscience and seek to be instructed by one better than yourself, rather than to follow your own inventions.

(5) READ THE SCRIPTURES

Read humbly, simply, honestly, and not desiring to win a character for learning. Ask freely and hear in silence the words of holy men; nor be displeased at the hard sayings of men older than yourself because they are not uttered without cause.

(6) LIVE MODERATELY

When a reasonable man desires more than his share he immediately becomes unbalanced and insecure.

(7) AVOID PRIDE

Don't assume you are better than the other man. God knoweth what is in man. The humble man finds peace in his heart.

(8) DON'T GET TOO FAMILIAR

Don't open your heart to every man, but deal with one who is wise and feareth God. We sometimes think we please others by our intimate conversation but immediately they begin to see the faults in our character and judge us.

(9) EXPLORE OPINION

Be careful whom you talk to. Don't insist on your opinion. Be open to listen to the opinions of others. "It is safer to hearken and to receive counsel than to give it."

(10) DON'T TALK TOO MUCH

If you must talk, say things which encourage people and help them to be better persons.

(11) SEEK PEACE OF MIND

Peace of mind comes from spiritual growth. We should go quickly on to perfection if each year we should see one fault rooted out from us.

(12) USE ADVERSITY

It is good for us that we sometimes have sorrows and adversities. They often make a man lay to heart that he is only a stranger and sojourner and may not put his trust in any worldly thing. It is good that we sometimes endure contradictions and are hardly and unfairly judged when we do and mean what is good, for these things help us to be humble and shield us from vain glory.

B. Jeremy Taylor

Three weeks after John Wesley had written to his mother that he was reading Thomas à Kempis, again at the suggestion of Betty Kirkham, he was seriously studying Jeremy Taylor. The volume, which first appeared as a unit in 1651, was divided into two parts. The first half discussed *The Rule and Exercise of Holy Living* (1650), the second *The Rule and Exercise of Holy Dying* (1651). John concerned himself with the first section of the book.

Jeremy Taylor, the author, gave to his discussion a richness which came from his own personal sufferings during his career. In 1635 Archbishop Laud appointed him to a fellowship in All Souls College, Oxford, but he was deprived of his living under the Commonwealth, being held as a prisoner in 1644. Retiring to Wales in 1645, he entered the productive literary period of his life. Upon the restoration in 1660 he was given a bishopric.

In dedicating his book to the Earl of Carberry, Taylor set out the characteristics of a Christian in a series of twelve propositions which subsequently became important in the work of John Wesley. A man certainly belongs to God, he said, who:

(1) "believes and is baptized into all the articles of Christian faith and studies to improve his knowledge in the manners of God so as best make him live a holy life
(2) "obeys Christ absolutely, worships God diligently, frequently, and constantly with natural religion—that is in expression of prayer, praise, and thanksgiving
(3) "takes all opportunity to remember Christ's death by a frequent sacrament or by inward acts of understanding of the will and in the memory of Christ which is the spiritual communion that supplies the want of the external rite
(4) "lives chastely
(5) "is merciful
(6) "despises the world
(7) "is just in his dealing and diligent in his callings
(8) "is humble in his spirit
(9) "is obedient to his government
(10) "is content in his fortune of employment
(11) "does his duty because he loves God
(12) "is prepared to suffer affliction for the cause of God."

Taylor was actually stating rules of personal religion which no power of man could deprive a Christian of. The rules, he pointed out, were plain, useful, and fitted for the best understanding. They were a prescription for spiritual health and persons who would profit by them must live "as if under a physician's hand." The rules, he felt, must be used like nourishment by daily care and meditation and not like a single medicine taken for a present necessity.

Taylor's literary method was effective. First he set forth the rule and then followed it by a discussion of the benefits to be derived from the exercise. He classified the means of serving the holy life into three instruments of holy living:

(1) Care of time
(2) Purity of intention
(3) Practice of the presence of God

Taylor set forth as his basic premise that every man was holy. Hence all his labors, care, powers, and facilities should be holy and employed in the service of God. To aid man to find this holiness he laid down three principles:

(1) TIME—a man should lay aside for the service of God and the business of the Spirit as much time as he can because God rewards minutes with long and eternal happiness.
(2) ATTITUDE—every minute of living is an opportunity to serve God.
(3) PRESENCE OF GOD—a man is continually standing before God, his judge in all his acting, speaking, and thinking.

(1) TIME

John Wesley was deeply impressed with Jeremy Taylor's discussion on the care of time as the first general instrument of holy living. Taylor said that God had given to man a short time here upon earth and yet upon the use of this short time eternity depends. "He who is choice of time," said Taylor, "will also be choice of company and his actions, lest the first engage him in vanity and loss, the latter by being criminal by throwing of himself and his time away by going back, in the accounts of eternity." "*Idleness,*" he continued, "is the greatest waste in the world; it throws away that which is invaluable and respective of use and irreparable when it is passed, unable to be recovered by art or by nature." "But remember," Taylor admonished, "we have a great work to do, many enemies to conquer, much evil to prevent, much danger to run through, many difficulties to be met, many necessities to be served, and much good to do." God has given every man work enough to do, and "there should be *no room for idleness and time for devotion.*" Taylor likened idleness to the funeral of a living man. Then he sets forth the rules for employing time:

(1) *In the morning* when you awaken accustom yourself to think upon God or something in order to His service. *At night* before you close your eyes, think upon God and sometimes watch the dawn or as he says, "the preparation the sun makes as he is coming forth from his chambers in the evening."

(2) Let every man be exhibited in the point of his employment.

(3) Let all the void spaces of time be spent in prayer, reading, meditating, works of nature, recreations, charity, friendliness and neighborhood and means of spiritual and corporal help. Begin and end the day with God and such forms of devotion as are proper.

(4) Don't let holidays and festivals be days of idleness. It is better to plow upon holy days than to spend time in idleness. Spend holidays in religion and charity according to the appointed rules.

(5) Avoid the company of drunkards and busybodies and all such. A man who is not provident in the use of his time is not prudent in the choice of his company.

(6) Never walk with any man or take any trifling appointment merely to pass away time. Every day well spent may become a day of salvation.

(7) In the midst of the work of your ordinary occupation retire to God for short prayers and ejaculations.

(8) Let your employment be such as may become a reasonable person. A man may be idly busy, said Taylor, and take great pains to such little purpose that his labors and expense of time shall serve no end but folly and vanity. There are some people who are busy, but "busy only in catching flies."

(9) Let your employment be fitted to your person and calling. Some people employ their time infinitely below the dignity of their person. Thus Nero went up and down Greece challenging the fiddlers at their trade. Aerpus made lanterns. Harcitious, King of Parthia, caught moles, and Biantes filed needles.

Following his intensive study of Jeremy Taylor's discussion of time, John Wesley wrote to his brother Samuel:

> "Leisure and I have taken leave of one another. I propose to be busy as long as I live if my health is so long indulged to me."

That decision was important for a university man of twenty-three. The next winter he confided to his mother:

> "I am full of business; but have found a way to write without taking any time from that. 'Tis rising an hour sooner in the morning and going into company an hour later in the evening; both of which may be done without any inconvenience."

Indeed, his diary showed the direct effect of Taylor's propositions for he wrote down in his journal these

General Rules of Employing Time

(1) Begin and end every day with God; sleep not immoderately.

(2) Be diligent in your calling.

(3) Employ all spare hours in religion, as able.

(4) All holidays (holy days).

(5) Avoid drunkards and busybodies.

(6) Avoid curiosity and all useless employments and knowledge.

(7) Examine yourself every night.

(8) Never on any account pass a day without setting aside at least an hour for devotion.

(9) Avoid all manner of passion.

(2) Purity of Intention

The general principle of "purity of intention" is this: "that we should intend and design God's glory in every action we do, whether it be natural or chosen." Paul in I Corinthians 10:31 stated it in these words:

Whether ye eat or drink, do all to the glory of God.

"Which rule," said Jeremy Taylor, "when we observe, every action of nature become religious, and every meal is an act of worship, and shall have its reward in its proportion, as well as an act of prayer."

True to his formula, Taylor reduced this general principle to working rules as follows:

(1) In every action reflect upon the end . . . In your undertaking it, consider why you do it, and what you propound to yourself for a reward, and to your action as its end.

(2) Begin every action in the name of the Father, of the Son, and of the Holy Ghost; meaning
   (a) that we do not the action without the permission or warrant of God.
   (b) that we design it to the glory of God, if not in the direct action, yet at least in its consequence.

(3) Begin every action with prayer that God will not only bless the action but "sanctify your purpose" and in presenting yourself to God know that "holy and well-intended actions" are the best presents you can make to God.

(4) Renew and re-enkindle your purpose in carrying out the action by short ejaculations such as:
   "Not unto us, O Lord, not unto us, but unto thy name let all praise be given."
   "Now I am working the work of God; I am his servant. I am in a happy employment. I am doing my Master's business. I am not at my own dispose. I am using his talents. All the gain must be his."

(5) Do not let an action well begun and intended for God's glory decline and end in your own praise or temporal satisfaction or a sin, or as Taylor says, "have a care that, while the altar thus sends up a holy fume, thou dost not suffer the birds to come and carry away the sacrifice."

(3) Practice of the Presence of God

Taylor's third proposition makes it clear that man lives in the presence of God who "is present in all places," "sees every action," "hears all discourses," and "understands every thought." As 17 Acts 28 says: "in Him we live, and move, and have our being." God, said Taylor, is everywhere by his essence and by his power. He is present in the hearts of his people for "the temple itself is the heart of man." He is especially present in the consciences of all persons by way of testimony and judgment. "God stands as a witness and judge . . . God is the great eye of the world, always watching over our actions, and an ever-open ear to hear all our words, and an unwearied arm ever lifted up to crush a sinner into ruin."

Taylor reduced the instrument of holy living to practice according to these rules:

(1) Let this actual thought often return, that God is omnipresent, filling every place. Say with David as in 139 Psalm 7-8, "Whither shall I go from thy Spirit, or whither shall I flee from thy presence?"
(2) Make an act of adoration in the beginning of actions. Place yourself in God's presence "for when thou hast placed yourself before him, and kneelest in his presence, it is most likely all the following parts of thy devotion will be answerable to the wisdom of such an apprehension, and the glory of such a presence."
(3) Carry on short dialogs and discussions between God and your own soul. "In the midst of the works of your trade, . . . retire into your chapel, your heart. Converse with God by frequent addresses and returns."
(4) Be cruel toward no person because "God is in every creature."
(5) Walk as in the presence of God by conversing with him in frequent prayer and frequent communion.

As a first prayer, Taylor wrote a petition to spend time well. It began:

> *O eternal God, who from all eternity dost behold and love thy own glories and perfections infinite, and hast created me to do the work of God after the manner of men, and to serve thee in this generation and according to my capacities; give me thy grace that I may be a curious and prudent spender of my time, so as I may best prevent or resist all temptation, and be profitable to the Christian commonwealth, and, by discharging all my duties, may glorify thy name.*

Taylor's plan for daily prayers ran like this:

MORNING—first prayers as soon as dressed

(1) "Humbly and reverently compose yourself, with heart lifted up to God, and your head bowed, and meekly kneeling upon your knees, say the Lord's Prayer: after which use . . . collects" such as

Holy, holy, holy, Lord God Almighty, who was, and is, and is to come; heaven and earth, angels and men, the air and sea, give glory, and honour, and thanks to him that sitteth on the throne, who liveth for ever and ever . . .

Sing praises unto the Lord. Give thanks to him for a remembrance of his holiness. Thou hast showed me marvelous great kindness, and hast blessed me for ever: the greatness of thy glory reachest unto the heavens, and thy truth unto the clouds. O my God, I will give thanks unto thee for ever. Hallelujah!

(2) Present yourself to God for the day.

Most holy and eternal God, I humbly present to thy Divine Majesty myself, my soul and body, my thoughts and words, my passions and my sufferings, to be disposed by thee to thy glory; to be blessed by thy providence; to be sanctified by thy spirit; to be guided by thy counsel. Thy day, O Lord, and all the days of my life, I dedicate to thy honour, and the actions of my calling to the uses of grace, and the religion of all my days to be united to the merits and intercession of my holy Saviour Jesus; that in him and for Him I may be pardoned and accepted. Amen.

(3) Repent.

Lord, pardon all my sins, for, as for me, I am not worthy to be called thy servant—I—a lover of the things of the world, and a despiser of the things of God; proud and envious, intemperate, impatient of reproof, desirous to seem holy, and negligent of being so; fooled with presumption and false principles; disturbed with anger . . .

Holy Jesus, save me and deliver me . . . O just and dear God, be gracious to thy servant.

(4) Intercede and pray for others.

O God of infinite mercy, who hast compassion on all men, and relievest the necessities of all that call to thee for help, hear the prayers of thy servant, who is unworthy to ask any petition for himself, yet, in humility and duty, is bound to pray for others . . . (Here make specific mention and need).

(6) Read and meditate upon some portion of the Holy Scriptures. Humbly composing yourself upon your knees, make ejaculations such as

My help standeth in the name of the Lord, who hath made heaven and earth.

Lord, hear the prayer of thy servant, and give me thy Holy Spirit.

(7) Pray for yourself.

Give me a tender conscience; a conversation discreet and affable, modest and patient, liberal and obliging . . . that I may be as thou wouldst have me. Amen.

Holy is our God. Holy is the Almighty. Holy, holy, holy Lord God, have mercy upon me.

EVENING

O Lord, pardon all my sins, my light and rash words, the vanity and impiety of my thoughts, my unjust and uncharitable actions, and whatsoever I have transgressed against thee this day, or at any time before. Teach me to walk always in thy presence. Let thy loving spirit guide me in the ways of peace and safety, that with the testimony of a good conscience, and the sense of thy mercies and refreshment I may advance thy glory. Amen.

BED-TIME

I will lift up my eyes unto the hills, from whence cometh my help. My help cometh of the Lord, which made heaven and earth. He will not suffer thy foot to be moved; he that keepeth thee will not slumber. Behold, he that keepeth Israel shall neither slumber nor sleep. The Lord is thy keeper; the Lord is thy shade upon thy right hand. The sun shall not smite thee by day, neither the moon by night. The Lord shall preserve thee from all evil; he shall preserve thy soul. The Lord shall preserve thy going out and thy coming in, from this time forth for evermore.

Glory be to the Father, etc.

— Prayer —

Bless my sleep unto me; a refreshment to my wearied body, to enable it to serve my soul that both may serve thee with a never-failing duty.

IN THE NIGHT WHEN AWAKE

Ejaculations and short meditations.

I will lay me down in peace and sleep; for thou, Lord, only makest me to dwell in safety.

> "Meditate on Jacob's wrestling with the angel all night; be thou also importunate with God for a blessing, and give not over till he hath blessed thee."

In recommending the devotional pattern, Taylor pointed out that all the forms he had recommended would require no more than ninety minutes a day—a small portion afforded to God out of twenty-four hours. He prescribed exercise for all kinds of daily operations from temperance in eating and drinking to humility.

His discussion of contentedness further shows his method. Because contentedness was the sum of all the old moral philosophy, and is of most universal use in the whole course of men's lives, the attitude becomes an instrument to ease the burden of the world and the enmities of sad chance. He considers being contented in all states a duty of religion. Said Taylor:

> "God is the master of the scenes; we must not choose which part we shall act; it concerns us only to be careful that we do it well, always saying, 'If this please God, let it be as it is!' And we . . . pray that God's will may be done in earth as it is in heaven."

As instruments or exercises to achieve contentedness, Taylor recommended:

(1) *Turn trouble to spiritual advantage.*

"When anything happens to our displeasure, let us endeavor to take off its trouble by turning it into spiritual advantage, and handle it on that side in which it may be useful to the design of reason; for there is nothing but hath a double handle, or at least we have two hands to apprehend it. When an enemy reproaches us, let us look on him as an impartial relater of our faults, for he will tell thee truer than thy fondest friend . . . If, therefore, thou fallest from thy employment in public take sanctuary in an honest retirement, being indifferent to thy gain abroad, or thy safety at home. If thou art out of favour with thy prince, secure the favour of the King of Kings, and then there is no harm come to thee. When Zeno Citiensis lost all his goods in a storm, he retired to the studies of philosophy, to his short cloak, and a severe life, and gave thanks to fortune for his prosperous mischance."

(2) *Never compare your position with those above you;*
rather look upon those thousands with whom you would not
for any interest change your fortune or condition.

"There is no wise or good man that would change persons or conditions entirely with any man in the world. It may be, he would have one man's wealth added to himself, or the power of a second, or the learning of a third; but still he would receive those into his own person because he loves that best, and therefore esteems it best, and therefore overvalues all that which he is, before all that which any other man in the world can be . . . For every man hath desires of his own, and objects just fitted to them, without which he cannot be unless he were not himself, and let every man that loves himself so well as to love himself before all the world, consider if he have not something for which in the whole world he values himself far more than he can value any man else. There is, therefore, no reason to take the finest feathers from all the winged nation to deck that bird that thinks already she is more valuable than any of the inhabitants of the air. Cease to love yourself best, or be content with that portion of being and blessing for which you love yourself so well."

(3) *Consider the better to blot out the worse.*

"It conduces much to our content, if we pass by those things which happen to our trouble, and consider that which is pleasing and prosperous, that, by the representation of the better, the worse may be blotted out; and, at the worst, you have enough to keep you alive, and to keep up and to improve your hopes of heaven, . . . or else please thyself with hopes of the future; for we were not born with this sadness upon us, and it was a change that brought us into it, and a change may bring us out again . . . It may be thou art entered into the cloud, which will bring a gentle shower to refresh thy sorrows . . . Thou art but a stranger travelling to thy country, where the glories of the kingdom are prepared for thee; it is therefore a huge folly to be much afflicted because thou hast a less convenient inn to lodge in by the way . . . These arts of looking forwards and backwards are more than enough to support the spirit of a Christian: there is no man but hath blessings enough in present possession to outweigh the evils of a great affliction."

(4) *Enjoy the present; don't worry about the future.*

"If you take your foot from the present standing, and thrust it forward towards tomorrow's event, you are in a restless condition: it is like refusing to quench your present thirst by fearing you shall want the drink the next day. Enjoy the blessings of this day, if God sends them, and the evils of it bear patiently and sweetly; for this day is only ours: we are dead to yesterday, and we are not yet born to the morrow. 'Sufficient to the day (said Christ) is the evil thereof.' Sufficient, but not intolerable."

(5) *Expect change.*

"Let us prepare our minds against changes, always expecting them, that we be not surprised when they come: for nothing is so great an enemy to tranquility and a contented spirit as the amazement and confusions of unreadiness and inconsideration; and when our fortunes are violently changed, our spirits are unchanged if they always stood in the suburbs and expectations of sorrows."

(6) *Count your blessings.*

"Let us often frame to ourselves, and represent to our considerations, the images of those blessings we have, just as we usually understand them when we want them. Consider how desirable health is to a sick man, or liberty to a prisoner; and if but a fit of toothache seizes us with violence, all these troubles which in our health afflicted us disband instantly, and seem inconsiderable . . . Remember, then, that God hath given thee a blessing, the want of which is infinitely more trouble than thy present debt, or poverty, or loss; and therefore is now more to be valued in the possession, and ought to outweigh thy trouble. The very privative blessings, the blessings of immunity, safeguard, liberty, and integrity, which we commonly enjoy, deserve the thanksgiving of a whole life . . . Thou art quit from a thousand calamities, every one of which, if it were upon thee, would make thee insensible of thy present sorrow; and therefore let thy joy (which should be as great for they freedom from them, as is thy sadness when thou feelest any of them) do the same cure upon thy discontent. For if we be not extremely foolish or vain, thankless or senseless, a great joy is more apt to cure sorrow and discontent than a great trouble is."

(7) *Be governed by your needs, not by your fancy.*

. . . Measure your desires by your fortune and condition, not your fortunes by your desires . . . He that would shoot an arrow out of a plough, or hunt a hare with an elephant, is not unfortunate for missing the mark or prey; but he is foolish for choosing such unapt instruments: and so is he that runs after his content with appetites not springing from natural needs, but from artificial, fantastical, and violent necessities. Is that heart better that hath two or three mountains to gaze on, than a little bee that feeds on dew or manna, and lives upon what falls every morning from the storehouses of heaven, clouds, and providence? Can a man quench his thirst better out of a river than a full urn, or drink better from the fountain which is finely paved with marble, than when it swells over the green turf?

(8) *Take sanctuary in religion.*

The greatest evils are from within us; and from ourselves, also, we must look for our greatest good; for God is the fountain of it, but reaches it to us by our own hands; and when all things look sadly round about us, then only we shall find how excellent a fortune it is to have God to be our friend and, of all friendships, that only is created to support us in our needs; for it is sin that turns an ague into a fever . . . fear into despair, anger into rage, and loss into madness, and sorrow to amazement and confusion. Let us not therefore be governed by external, and present, and seeming things; . . . Let reason, and experience, and religion, and hope relying upon the Divine promises, be the measure of our judgment. No wise man did ever think virtue could depend upon the variety of a good or bad fortune.

The systematic method of Jeremy Taylor runs throughout the book. His treatment of the three enemies of mercifulness again shows how he organized his materials and reduced his principles to exercises which can be used by people on Main Street and Bye Street. The three enemies are (1) envy, (2) anger, and (3) covetousness. Let us look at the way he handles anger as a treatment typical of his discussion of both envy and covetousness.

Disease	*Remedy*
Anger	
	(1) *Pray; lay aside your emotion and address God.*
	(2) *Seal your lips.*
	(3) *Be humble. "Humility is the most excellent natural cure for anger; for he that, by daily considering his own infirmities and failings, makes the error of his neighbor or servant to be his own case, and remembers that he daily needs God's pardon and his brother's charity, will not be apt to rage at the levities, or misfortunes, or indiscretions of another greater than which he considers that he is very frequently and more inexcusably guilty of. Consider the example of the ever blessed Jesus, who suffered all the contradictions of sinners, and received all affronts and reproaches of malicious, rash, and foolish persons, and yet in all of them was as dispassionate and gentle as the morning sun in autumn; and in this also he propounded himself imitable by us."*

C. William Law

The third book which influenced John Wesley during his formative years was the popular devotional volume entitled *The Treatise of Christian Perfection* (1726) by William Law. Law, the son of a Petersborough grocer and chandler, entered Emmanuel College and took his Master of Arts degree from Cambridge. Taking holy orders, he resigned his fellowship when he found himself conscientiously unable to swear allegiance to George I and to adjure the Stuart pretender. As a result of this decision he was barred from holding any University office or church appointment. Looking for employment, he became the tutor of Edward Gibbon, the father of the distinguished historian.

Law followed this volume with a second which greatly influenced the Methodist tradition. It was called *A Serious Call* which reinforced the ideas of Jeremy Taylor in John Wesley's mind. Among Law's basic propositions were these:

(1) Fix it deep in your mind that you have but one business upon your hands: to seek for eternal happiness by doing the will of God.

(2) Avoid all concern of the world.

(3) Be assured that greatness of human nature consists in nothing else but in imitating the divine nature.

(4) Avoid all idleness.

(5) Think humbly of yourself and with great charity of all others.

Law defined devotion as "a life given or devoted to God." He specified the characteristics of the "devout man" as one "who lives no longer to his own will, or the way and spirit of the world, but to the sole will of God; who considers God in everything; who serves God in everything, who makes all the parts of his common life parts of piety by doing everything in the name of God and under such rules as are conformable to His glory." To Law the first and most fundamental principle of Christianity is always "an intention to please God in all our actions."

The two special devices which Law used to emphasize the character and method of the devout life were *word character portraits* of representative types of upper class people and *specific routines* for the cultivation of holy living.

Word Portraits

Law used the technique of word portraits to analyze character. His purpose was to show the absurd contradictions in human action and to make vivid by examples representative inconsistencies in human behavior. By this method he sought to convince in the plainest manner that the strictest rules of religion, far from rendering life dull and uncomfortable, actually contributed to the full life. "Want of religion," he said, "made life dull and purposeless."

Giving his representative characters Latin names, Law by his ingenious method was able to be concrete without giving offense to specific persons. His word portraits were descriptions of living people we meet every day. We see ourselves.

Among his people were for example:

CAECUS —*haughty and imperious to inferiors, always right and bearing no contradiction, the rich man of good birth and fine points who admires humility and hates pride in other people*

CAELIA —*the rich woman who goes around telling always "how provoked she is, what 'intolerable, shocking' things are always happening to her, and what vexations she meets with everywhere"*

CALIDUS —*the richer trader who buries the end of every long day's work at the tavern and spends his week-ends in idleness and refreshment*

CLASSICUS —*man of learning, versed in the best authors of antiquity, conversant with the best philosophers, man of taste and judgment, imitator of the models of life of classic men, reader of his testaments in Greek and no other books of devotion in his study, thinker of devotion as a form of repeating words, never as a state of the heart or the improvable state of the mind formed by the regular and diligent use of proper means*

COGNATUS —*sober, orthodox, regular clergyman, financially "sharp" on market prices, who lives to accumulate a fortune for his niece*

EUSEBIA —*the pious, well-born widow, mother of five daughters, who with her maids and daughters keeps all the hours of prayer, chants the psalms, does good works, follows innocent diversions, and lives plain, unaffected, sincere, and humble life*

FELICIANA —*a finely-dressed woman who revels in every new dress or diversion which comes to town*

FLATUS —*the rich, healthy man, always searching after health and happiness, always following a new project, trying to find something more worth his while*

FLAVIA —*sister of Miranda, woman with an income, concerned with the forms of religion and the values of the world*

FULVIUS —*an idle, independent, university-educated man, skeptical, "wise," making no pretense to piety, living as he pleases*

JULIUS —*man fearful of missing prayers but otherwise devoting himself to idleness and folly*

MATILDA —*fine woman of good breeding, common sense, and much religion—with a zeal for finery, concern for diet as related to figure, and preservation of complexion as evidence of age, whose three daughters turned out badly, one eloping with a gambler, and one dying at twenty from over-diet*

MIRANDA —*sister of Flavia, concerned with the spirit of religion and the values of her Lord*

MUNDANUS —*a perennially young elderly and powerful business figure of sound judgment, orderly and systematic mind, a perfectionist in all his operations except devotions, where he continued to use the methods and prayer in the form of little words his mother taught him to repeat morning and night when he was six, never having applied his genius for methods to improvement of his devotional life*

NEGOTIUS —*a powerful business man, community leader—sober, rich, prudent, prosperous, generous, charitable, donor of bells to the church, but with no time for inward solid piety and therefore living to what end*

OCTAVIUS —*a learned, ingenious man, well-versed in literature, traveled in Europe, linguist, who died bored, before his maid could bring him a fresh glass of wine*

SUCCUS —*man enjoying life made up of resting in bed and eating good meals when he was up, afraid he may catch cold, and counting all hours not given to repose or nourishment wasted*

SUSURRUS —*a pious, temperate, good man of excellent qualities who sees, hears, and discovers defects in all the persons about him*

This method deserves to be illustrated by the study of a full-length portrait. Take the case of Calidus, for example, an English business man, not just an eighteenth century figure, but one we all meet and know.

> "Calidus has traded above thirty years in the greatest city of the kingdom; he has been so many years constantly increasing his trade and his fortune. Every hour of the day is with him an hour of business; and though he eats and drinks very heartily, yet every meal seems to be in a hurry, and he would say grace if he had time. Calidus ends every day at the tavern, but has not leisure to be there till near nine o'clock.

"He is always forced to drink a good hearty glass, to drive thoughts of business out of his head and make his spirits drowsy enough for sleep. He does business all the time that he is rising, and has settled several matters before he can get to his counting-room. His prayers are a short ejaculation or two, which he never misses in stormy, tempestuous weather, because he has always something or other at sea. Calidus will tell you, with great pleasure, that he has been in this hurry for so many years, and that it must have killed him long ago, but that it has been a rule with him to get out of town every Saturday, and make Sunday a day of quiet and good refreshment in the country.

"He is now so rich that he would leave off his business, and amuse his old age with building and furnishing a fine house in the country, but that he is afraid he should grow melancholy if he were to quit his business. He will tell you with great gravity, that it is a dangerous thing for a man that has been used to get money, ever to leave it off. If thoughts of religion happen at any time to steal into his head, Calidus contents himself with thinking that he never was a friend to heretics and infidels, that he has always been civil to the minister of his parish, and very often given something to the charity schools."

Then there is the case of Flavia.

"Thus lives Flavia; and if she lives ten years longer, she will have spent about fifteen hundred and sixty Sundays after this manner. She will have worn about two hundred different suits of clothes. Out of these thirty years of her life, fifteen will have been disposed of in bed; and, of the remaining fifteen, about fourteen will have been consumed in eating, drinking, dressing, visiting, conversation, reading and hearing plays and romances, at operas, assemblies, balls and diversions. For you may reckon all the time that she is up, thus spent, except about an hour and a half, that is disposed of at church, most Sundays in the year. With great management, and under mighty rules of economy, she will have spent sixty hundred pounds upon herself, bating only some shillings, crowns, or half-crowns, that have gone from her in accidental charities . . . If you have seen her delighted in plays and romances, in scandal and backbiting, easily flattered, and soon affronted; if you have seen her devoted to pleasures and diversions, a slave to every passion in its turn, nice in everything that might benefit her soul, always wanting some new entertainment, and ready for every invention in show or dress, it was because she had purchased all these tempers with the yearly revenues of her fortune.

"She might have been humble, serious, devout, a lover of good books, an admirer of prayer and retirement, careful of time, diligent in good works, full of charity and the love of God, but that the imprudent use of her estate forced all the contrary tempers upon her."

From this critique of living people, Law turned to a consideration of "method." He began with prayer and he observed that "praying differs from saying prayers." He made suggestions on how to pray such as these:

(1) Have a prayer place—*as far as you can, always the same place; your chapel even if only a part of a room*

(2) Prepare yourself by singing—*not reading—a psalm*

(3) Kneel

(4) Shut your eyes

(5) Keep a short silence—*let your soul place itself in the presence of God*

(6) Begin with words expressive of God's greatness and power to raise your heart in worship and adoration—*use words which speak of God in the highest terms and most fully express his power, presence, and providence.*

(7) Have some fixed subject which becomes the chief concern of your prayer at a particular time of day.

To explain what he meant by a fixed subject for a particular time of day, he outlined a prayer calendar, pointing out that *"devotion is nothing else but right apprehension of God and right affection towards him" and that prayer is the nearest approach to God, and "the highest enjoyment of Him that we are capable of in this life."*

His daily prayer schedule ran like this:

Hour	Subject
6:00 A.M.	Thanksgiving and presenting ourselves to God (oblation) *Early rising exercises the will power and awakens the soul as none who arise by chance can experience*
9:00 A.M.	Humility *"Remember . . . there is but one man in the world with whom you have perpetual contention and he always striving to exceed him, and that is yourself."* *"Go through all the actions and accidents of life calmly and quietly, as in the presence of God: neither seeking vain applause nor resenting neglects or affronts, but doing and receiving everything in the meek and lowly spirit of our Lord and Saviour Jesus Christ."*
12:00 NOON	Universal love and intercession *Intercession means praying to God and interceding with Him for our fellow-creatures. Our Lord recommended His love to us as the pattern and example of our love to one another. As He continually makes intercession for us all, so ought we to intercede and pray for one another.* *"Nothing makes us love a man so much as praying for him; and when you can once do this sincerely for any man, you have fitted your soul for the performance of everything that is kind and civil towards him. By considering yourself an advocate with God for your neighbors and acquaintances you never find it hard to be at peace with them yourself. Prayers for others alter and amend the state of your own heart."* *"God is love; and he that dwelleth in love dwelleth in God, and God in him."* 1 John 4:16 *Intercessory prayer should state specific requests for the help of specific persons.* *Prayer is the best antidote in the world for the poison of human misunderstanding.*
3:00 P.M.	Resignation and conformity to the will of God *Thankfully receive and fully approve of everything that by order of God's providence happens to you.*

6:00 P.M. Examination, review, and account

At the end of your working day inspect and examine yourself, and review all the actions of the day so that you will not overlook the particular mistakes of the day and can amend your ways. Consider especially your chief frailty to which your nature most inclines you.

BEDTIME Justification of life

What reason have you for being alive tomorrow?
What good reason by the use of your life justifies God's mercy in letting you awaken in the morning?

Law concluded that

> *"there is nothing wise or great or noble in a human spirit but rightly to know and heartily to worship and to adore the Great God that is the support and life of all spirits."*

John Wesley absorbed the ideas of à Kempis, Taylor, and Law. As an Oxford man he practiced their suggestions, and, always given to practical methods of personal application, devised schedules and systems for self-appraisal in terms of standards.

Here, for example, is a questionnaire which he developed for applying the Great Commandment to his own needs:

PPLICATION OF THE GREAT COMMANDMENT

LOVE OF GOD

HAVE I

		Yes	*No*
(1)	been simple in everything I said or did?	☐	☐
(2)	done nothing except with a previous perception of its being the will of God?	☐	☐
(3)	prayed with fervor:		
	(a) at going in and out of church?	☐	☐
	(b) in the church?	☐	☐
	(c) morning and evening in private?	☐	☐
	(d) Monday, Wednesday, and Friday with my friends?	☐	☐
	(e) at rising?	☐	☐
	(f) before lying down?	☐	☐
	(g) on Saturday noon?	☐	☐
	(h) all the time I was engaged in exterior work?	☐	☐
	(i) in private?	☐	☐
	(j) before I went into the place of public or private prayer for help therein?	☐	☐
(4)	duly prayed for the virtue of the day—deliberately, seriously, fervently?	☐	☐
(5)	daily used ejaculations, prayed every hour for humility, faith, hope, love?	☐	☐
(6)	used a collect at 9, 12, and 3, and grace before and after eating? aloud at my own room, deliberately, seriously, fervently?	☐	☐
(7)	daily meditated		
	(a) from 6, etc. to prayers?	☐	☐
	(b) from 4 to 5 what was the particular in the providence of the day?	☐	☐
	(c) how did the virtue of the day fall short?	☐	☐
	(Here list faults)		
	i		
	ii		
	iii		
	iv		
	(d) on Sunday from 6 to 7 with Kempis?	☐	☐

		Yes	No
	(e) from 3 to 4 on redemption or God's attributes?	☐	☐
	(f) Wednesday and Friday from 12 to 1 on the Passion?	☐	☐
	(g) after ending a book on what I had marked in it?	☐	☐

LOVE OF MAN

Have I

		Yes	*No*
(1)	embraced every probable opportunity of doing good?	☐	☐
(2)	embraced every probable opportunity of preventing, removing, or lessening evil?	☐	☐
(3)	thought anything too dear to part with to serve my neighbor?	☐	☐
(4)	spent an hour at least every day in speaking to some one or other?	☐	☐
(5)	given any one up till he expressly renounced me?	☐	☐
(6)	before I spoke to any, learned as far as I could his temper, way of thinking, past life, and peculiar hindrance, internal and external, with definitions to be aimed at and then the means to it?	☐	☐
(7)	in speaking proposed the motives, then the difficulties?	☐	☐
(8)	persuade all I could to attend public prayers, sermons, and sacraments?	☐	☐
(9)	in disputing (1) desired my opponent to define the terms of the questions; to limit it; what he grants, what denies; delayed speaking my opinion; let him explain and prove his; then insinuated and pressed objections?	☐	☐
(10)	after every visit asked him who went with me: did I say anything wrong?	☐	☐
(11)	when anyone asked advice directed and exhorted him with all my power?	☐	☐
(12)	acted in good will with all my actions toward others?	☐	☐
(13)	have I daily used intercession		
	(a) before speaking to any?	☐	☐
	(b) after speaking to any?	☐	☐
	(c) for my friends on Sunday?	☐	☐
	(d) for my pupils on Monday?	☐	☐
	(e) for those who have particularly desired it on Wednesday and Friday?	☐	☐
	(f) for the family in which I am every day?	☐	☐

IX

ACADEMIC VOLUNTEERS

While chairman of a parliamentary investigating committee, James Edward Oglethorpe developed an interest in the English debtor class. Oglethorpe's study prompted him in 1732 to obtain a charter to establish an asylum for unfortunate people in America in the country lying between the Savannah and Altamaha rivers. He named the proposed colony *Georgia* to honor George II under whose auspices the project had been undertaken.

Oglethorpe's proposal excited public interest. When the trustees called for voluntary help, people donated money, Bibles, testaments, devotional and horn books, and furniture. John Burton, brilliant don of Oxford's Corpus Christi College and a trustee of the colony, preached and published a sermon in support of the project entitled *The Duty and ReWard of Propagating Principles of Religion and Virtue exemplified in the History of Abraham.* Samuel Wesley, Jr., was thrilled by the concept of the colony. Not only did he contribute five pounds, five shillings in the first public subscription to support the project, he also presented a "pewter chalice and patine for use in Georgia until silver ones were had." He composed his enthusiasm in a poem entitled *Georgia.* It read:

> See where beyond the spacious ocean lies
> A wide waste land beneath the southern skies;
> Where kindly suns for ages roll'd in vain,
> Nor e'er the vintage saw, or rip'ning grain;
> Where all things into wild luxuriance ran,

And burden'd Nature ask'd the aid of man.
In this sweet climate and prolific soil
He bids the eager swain indulge his toil;
In thee possession to the planter's hand
Consigns the rich uncultivated land.
"Go you," the Monarch cries, "go settle there,
Whom Britain from her plentitude can spare;
Go, your old wonted industry pursue,
Nor envy Spain the treasures of Peru."

Be not content in council here to join;
A farther labour, Oglethorpe, is thine.
In each great deed thou claim'st the foremost part,
And toil and danger charm thy generous heart.
But chief for this thy warm affections rise,
For O thou view'st it with a parent's eyes!
For this thou tempt'st the vast, tremendous main,
And floods and storms oppose their threats in vain.

He comes, whose life, when absent from your view,
Was one continued ministry for you;
For you were laid out all his plans and art,
Won every will, and soften'd every heart.
With what paternal joy shall he relate
How views its mother-isle your little state!
Think, while he strove your distant coast to gain,
How oft he sigh'd, and chid the tedious main!
Impatient to survey, by culture graced,
Your dreary woodland, and your rugged waste.
Fair were the scenes he feign'd the prospect fair;
And sure, ye Georgians, all he feign'd was there.
A thousand pleasures crowd into his breast;
But one, one mighty thought absorbs the rest,—
"And give me, Heaven, to see," the patriot cries,
"Another Britain in the desert rise."

With nobler products see thy Georgia teems,
Cheer'd with the genial sun's director beams;
There the wild vine to culture learns to yield,
And purple clusters ripen through the field.

Now bid thy merchants bring thy wine no more,
Or from the' Iberian or the Tuscan shore;
No more they need the' Hungarian vineyards drain,
And France herself may drink her best champagne.
Behold at last, and in a subject-land,
Nectar sufficient for thy large demand!

Delicious nectar, powerful to improve
Our hospitable mirth, and social love.
This for thy jovial sons. Nor less the care
Of thy young province to oblige the fair.
Here tend the silk-worm, in the verdant shade.

Samuel, Jr., wrote another poem entitled *An Ode to James Oglethorpe, Esq., in the Country.* And in admiration for achievements of Oglethorpe's Parliamentary Committee, Samuel wrote still another poem entitled *The Prisons Opened: a Poem, occasioned by the Glorious Proceedings of the Committee of the House of Commons, appointed to inquire into the State of the Jails of this Kingdom, in the year* 1728. In part it read:

What various paths unhappy mortals tread,
Which down to dungeons and to tortures lead!
In jail a few secure their ill-got store;
By vices many fall, by folly more . . .

Yet, Britain, cease thy captives' woes to mourn,
To break their chains, see Oglethorpe was born! . . .

Proceed, disinterested few, proceed,
Heal every wound, and succour every need;
Let all Britannia's misery be redressed;
Cite every tyrant, to the righteous test,
The test which innocence can never fear,
Candid though strict, impartial though severe.

Oglethorpe and the Wesley family had long been on intimate terms. He corresponded with Samuel Wesley, Sr., at the Epworth Rectory and generally assisted him in his pecuniary difficulties. Samuel Wesley, Jr., who merited the statesman's high regard, addressed the poems to him. John solicited and obtained support from him to assist in the publication of Father Wesley's lifetime literary labor entitled *Dissertationes in Librum Jobi.* When Oglethorpe returned after fifteen months from his first voyage to Georgia, to arrange for the second emigration, he naturally turned to the Wesley brothers at Oxford to help him in his project. In the summer of 1732, John was chosen a member of the *Society for the Propagation of Christian Knowledge.* This increased his interest in missions and two years later when he was in London on a literary commission for his father, he found a growing interest in the Georgia colony. The trustees in London were searching for persons to go to America to preach the gospel to the settlers and Indians. Oglethorpe knew well the Wesley brothers and when Dr. Burton brought Oglethorpe and John together in the city, they made it clear that John and his Oxford associates were needed on the other side of the ocean. When he was pressed to accept appointment to Georgia, John flatly refused. He said that the assignment would bring grief to his aged mother. Asked whether he would go if his mother consented, John suggested that the men sound her out. The inquiry was made after his father's death. The widowed mother replied: "Had I twenty sons, I should rejoice that they were all so employed, though I should never see them more."

A. Life Work Decision

When John returned to Oxford, he was faced with a series of issues deeply affecting his personal life and career. The summer and fall of 1734 was critical in his experience. He was thirty-one years of age. In July he had terminated the romance with Mary Granville which for four years had flourished chiefly by John's correspondence and hopes. In November a letter from his father forced him to reconsider his life plans. Behind all the issues lay the active invitation to go to America as a missionary.

His father, fast failing in health, had urged John to succeed him and accept the living at Epworth to preserve the fruits of his forty years of labor and on account of the "dear love and longing which this poor people has for you." Wesley had expected to remain in the academic life which he found so congenial. Now, his romance broken, he was in the same year faced with reconsidering his whole life plan. He took twenty days to answer his father's letter. Taking up his quill pen, he began:

> "The authority of a parent and the call of Providence are things of so sacred a nature that a question in which these are any way concerned deserve the most serious consideration."

John examined the pros and cons of the Epworth opportunity, arguing back and forth with himself. The answer to the question in his mind turned on a single point:

> "Whether I am to prefer a college life or that of a rector of a parish."

In a logic which could only lead him to do what he wanted to do—remain at Oxford—John started out with two propositions that

(1) "the glory of God and the different degrees of promoting it are to be our sole consideration and direction in the choice of any course of life," and
(2) the "course of life tends to the glory of God wherein we can most promote holiness in ourselves and others."

"When two ways of life are prepared," he continued in his letter to his father, "I should choose to begin with that part of the question, 'Which of these have I rational ground to believe will conduce most to my own improvement?' And that not only because it is every physician's concern to heal himself first, but because it seems we may judge with more ease, and perhaps certainty too, in which state we can most promote holiness in ourselves than in which we can most promote it in others." By holiness John meant a "complex habit of lowliness, meekness, purity, faith, hope, and the love of God and man," qualities which he had increasingly associated with religion since Betty Kirkham influenced him to read Thomas à Kempis, Jeremy Taylor, and William Law way back in the spring of 1725. He came to the conclusion that Oxford was the locality where he, John Wesley, could best promote the holiness of John Wesley, Lincoln College tutor. His reasons were these:

(1) because in Oxford he could daily converse with friends and "I know of no other place under heaven where I can have always at hand half a dozen persons nearly of my own judgment and engaged in the same studies . . . To have such a number of friends constantly watching over my soul, and according to the variety of occasions administering reproof, advice, or exhortation with all plainness and all gentleness, is a blessing I have not yet found any Christians to enjoy in any other part of the kingdom."

(2) because in Oxford he could enjoy a degree of retirement as he pleased. He could have as much or as little company as he pleased

(3) because in Oxford he had the blessing of useful and uninterrupted freedom from trifling acquaintances

(4) because in Oxford, next to the advantage to freedom from useless and therefore hurtful company, he had no cares of the world. His income was ready for him on pay day. All he had to do was to carry the money to his room and count it. His

food was provided without any care on his part. "I have nothing to do but at such an hour to take and eat what is prepared for me. My laundress, barber, &c., are always ready at quarter-day." In short, conditions were so favorable that he was able to carry out the injunction of Paul that a man for his own profit should be able to "attend upon the Lord without distraction."

(5) because he had the opportunity of public prayer twice a day and of weekly communicating.

It was pretty clear that John liked Oxford and intended to stay there! He then proceeded to demolish the arguments advanced by his father in favor of his move to Epworth. To the argument that Epworth with its two thousand souls offered a "larger sphere of action," John replied that he did not see how any living man could "take care of an hundred." To the argument that the people of Epworth loved him, John asked his father how much these same people loved him at first and how they had treated him since! And what had his father done for so many years that had not been better done by men in Oxford? John felt that the Good Shepherd who took care of the poor sheep at Epworth before his father was born would not "forget them" when Samuel, Sr., was dead.

To his brother, Samuel, Jr., who felt that he should go to Epworth, John pointed out that he was more useful at Oxford because it is "a more extensive benefit to sweeten the fountain than to do the same to particular streams." And to Samuel's suggestion that "the tutor who being in Orders and never accepting a parish is perjured," John made a total denial, being too kind to say his brother Samuel, having taken orders, had not taken a parish. He felt that a clergyman should live where he could best serve God and his Church; he told his brother he could do this better at Oxford than at Epworth.

No one can read the record without the feeling that the life of such a self-satisfied and self-centered young bachelor ought to be disturbed. The substance of John's position, stripped of its religious vocabulary, was merely that a young man must decide his own goals and pursue them in his own ways. *It is his life that is being lived.* Every young person faces this tug of obligation to parents. He collides as well with the ideas of the way he should live his life as brothers and sisters would like to see him live it. Time, which Jeremy Taylor had described in such detail, sweeps human beings forward, bringing young men and women to their maturity. Parents age. Death of parents widens the dimensions to young experience as life, heretofore lived in the present and in planning for tomorrow, suddenly discovers a yesterday filled with the warm and vivid memories of parental affection and family living. John Wesley was witnessing the end of his father's career; he was on the threshold of his own. And now he stood alone at a forking of the roads where *he* was going to make a choice that affected the rest of the fifty-six years of his life. He had to choose which of three roads he would travel. Already he had made a series of decisions. In London he had refused point blank to go to Georgia with Oglethorpe. In the letters to his father he had made his position perfectly clear that he intended to remain in the delightful and convenient environment of Lincoln College, Oxford. Further, when Oglethorpe arrived back in England from Georgia in the summer of 1734, Samuel, Sr., in failing health but still warm in his concern for human welfare, wrote the Governor a letter. Calling him a "Universal Benefactor of Mankind," the Rector said: "It is not only your valuable favours on many accounts to my son, late of Westminster, and myself, when I was not a little pressed in the world, nor your more extensive charity to the poor prisoners." What Samuel, Sr., felt most important was Oglethorpe's "disinterested and immovable attachment" to his country, his raising a new colony, or rather a little world of his own in the midst of wild woods and uncultivated deserts.

As springtime came in 1735, the condition of Samuel Wesley, Sr., became worse. He had failed to influence his son, Samuel, to take steps to secure the next presentation to the Epworth living. Samuel, Sr., and Samuel, Jr., had together been unsuccessful in influencing John to succeed his father. And the rectory where John had been born thirty-two years before, which by his decision might continue to be a home for his mother, was about to pass away as the center of Wesley living. When their father's illness became critical, John and Charles hastened from Oxford to Epworth to be at his bedside in his last hours. His strength had been exhausted by sustained application in finishing his learned Latin treatise on the Book of Job. Since the summer of 1734, feeling the shortness of time, he had pressed hard to get off the copy for his book and had obtained subscriptions, including one for nine copies from Oglethorpe, to pay for the paper, printing, and maps. John was supervising the remainder of the work on trips to London. An artist, living at the Epworth rectory, was engraving and working off the remaining maps and figures. The father looked forward to having the project completed and to delivering copies in person in London the next year. But he was failing rapidly. At death his spirit was at peace with the world. Looking at his son, John, the father said softly:

> "The inward witness, son, the inward witness; this is the proof, the strongest proof, of Christianity."

To Charles he said:

> "Be steady. The Christian faith will surely revive in this kingdom. You shall see it, though I shall not."

Together John and Charles witnessed the passing of their first parent. This is one of the most earth-shattering and maturing experiences of life.

The life-time literary work of Samuel, Sr., came from the press after his death. The Epworth Rector had dedicated it by permission to Queen Caroline. In the early fall of 1735 John went to London to present a copy of the *Latin Dissertationes in Librum Jobi* to her Majesty. As John waited to meet the Queen, he remembered his father's devotion to the writing of this volume. When he was introduced, the Queen was romping with her maids of honor. She stopped her play for a moment, listened to him graciously. When John made the presentation on bended knee, Queen Caroline looked at the cover and responded: "It is very prettily bound." Her Majesty laid it down on a window ledge without opening a page. John Wesley, Oxford don, rose from his knees, bowed, and retired. The Queen bowed, smiled, spoke a few kind words, and resumed her sport. Ten days later John and Charles Wesley, together, were on the Atlantic sailing for Georgia. John had made his decision.

B. Mission to Georgia

On September 8, 1735, John Burton, the brilliant don of Corpus Christi College, who had brought John and Oglethorpe together in London months before, wrote to John:

> "Your short conference with Mr. Oglethorpe has raised the hopes of many good persons that you and yours would join in an undertaking which cannot be better executed than by such instruments."

Ten days later Dr. Burton wrote again. He said:

> "'Tis a happy circumstance that you should offer yourselves on this occasion. May your hands be strengthened and your endeavors prospered!"

John had chosen the third road. He was outbound to become a missionary to the Indians under the sponsorship of the *Society for the Propagation of the Gospel In Foreign Parts.* Charles, who regularly had declined to enter holy orders, now accepted appointment as secretary to Governor Oglethorpe. In a new spirit, he was anxious to be ordained so that he could officiate in the colony where the spiritual interests of the people had been neglected for want of clergymen. He was ordained a deacon in the Church of England on September 21, 1735. Eight days later Bishop Potter ordained him a priest with ceremonies in the Cathedral of Christ Church and in the presence of his brother, John, who had taken his orders in the same Cathedral and from the same Bishop just seven years before.

Four days before the brothers boarded the ship for America John wrote to Dr. Burton. Reversing himself on reasons why he should remain at Oxford, he referred to the "hope of doing more good in America." But "Why?" he asked. He answered his own question, still conducting a dialog with himself: "For the very plain reason: because these heathen at home have Moses and the Prophets, and those have not; because these who *have* the gospel trample upon it, and those who have it not earnestly call for it; 'therefore, seeing these judge themselves unworthy of eternal life, lo, I turn to the Gentiles.' "

John was still concerned with saving his own soul; out of the Oxford environment he expected he would find new spiritual strength in missionary action. He wrote to Dr. Burton:

"I hope to learn the true sense of the gospel of Christ by preaching it to the heathen. They have no comments to construe away the text; no vain philosophy to corrupt it; no luxurious, sensual, covetous, ambitious expounders to soften its unpleasing truths, to reconcile earthly-mindedness and faith, the Spirit of Christ, and the spirit of the world. They have no party, no interest to serve, and are therefore fit to receive the gospel in its simplicity. They are as little children, humble, willing to learn, and eager to do the will of God; and consequently they shall know of every doctrine I preach whether it be of God. By these, therefore, I hope to learn the purity of faith which was once delivered to the saints."

However much John may have overestimated the response of the American Indians to his preaching, he was most certainly convinced of the possibilities of his mission. Accompanied by Dr. Burton the brothers traveled to Gravesend to embark for Georgia.

Less than a month after Charles had taken orders as a priest of the Church of England, two brothers as ordained clergymen climbed aboard the ship *Simmonds* and went to their cabin in the forecastle. The next day John wrote to his brother, Samuel, urging him to instruct his students, "not only in the beggarly elements of Greek and Latin, but much more in the gospel." "Convince your students," he exhorted his brother, that "Christianity is not a negation or an external thing, but a new heart, a mind conformed to that of Christ, 'faith working by love.' . . . Pray for us."

Before the *Simmonds* sailed, John began to learn German so that he could converse with the twenty-six Moravians on board who, as Wesley noted in his diary, "left all for their Master, and who have indeed learned of Him, being meek and lowly, dead to the world, full of faith and of the Holy Ghost."

Saturday morning, while the ship still stood at anchor in the harbor, John arose as usual at four-thirty o'clock, made his prayers, read the sixth chapter of Genesis

> "when men began to multiply on the face of the earth, and daughters were born unto them . . . they took them wives . . . There were giants in the earth in those days; and also after that . . ."

Dipping his quill pen, he wrote to Betty Kirkham. The next day was Sunday. He arose at four-thirty and by seven o'clock was reading Thomas à Kempis, the volume which Betty Kirkham had recommended to him in the springtime of his undergraduate days in Christ Church ten years before. Sunday evening he joined with the Moravians on the deck to sing with them Paul Gerhardt's classic *Befiehl du deine Wege*:

> *Through waves and clouds and storms*
> *He gently clears the way.*

His contact with the Moravians opened his British soul to the rich German evangelical experience. During the Georgia years he translated thirty-three hymns from German into English. One of these was Gerhardt's O *Jesu Christ, mein schonstes Licht*:

> *In suffering be Thy love my peace,*
> *In weakness be Thy love my power.*